IN HER FOOTSTEPS

101 Remarkable Black Women

from the Queen of Sheba to Queen Latifah

ANNETTE MADDEN

CONARI PRESS
Berkeley, California

Conari Press books are distributed by Publishers Group West.

Cover illustration: detail from "Promenade II" © Rae Louise Hayward
Interior illustrations: details from "Sisters United Five" © Rae Louise Hayward
Cover design: Jeanette Madden
Cover art direction: Ame Beanland
Book design: Claudia Smelser
Author photo: Don McIlraith

Library of Congress Cataloging-in-Publication Data

Madden, Annette.
    In her footsteps : 100 remarkable Black women from the Queen of Sheba to Queen Latifah / Annette Madden.
        p.   cm.
        Includes bibliographical references and index.
        ISBN 1-57324-553-4
        1. Women, Black—Biography. 2. Afro-American women—Biography. I. Title.
CT3235 .M33 2000
920.72'089'96073—dc21   00-010692

Printed in the United States of America on recycled paper.
00 01 02 03 DATA 10 9 8 7 6 5 4 3 2 1

IN HER FOOTSTEPS

INTRODUCTiON

ONE DAY AN Ethiopian woman, approximately twenty-five years old and only 3 feet 6 inches tall, died for unknown reasons. Parts of her skeleton were found 3.2 million years later, and she was dubbed "Lucy"—the first woman in the world—according to the archeological record. Her Ethiopian descendants named her Dinknesh, which means "You are lovely." Who she was, what she did, and how she died is shrouded in mystery. Not so with her descendants who are described in this book.

This book is a gathering of profiles of women of African ancestry, from around the world and throughout time. Although a few of the women included in this book will be well known to you, I have purposely tried to include many less well-known women whose stories should be told for two reasons: one is that tracking down information on these wonderful Black women has been an adventure; and the other is that many of the well-known women have been written about ad infinitum. Not that the well-known ones aren't worthy of the attention—it's just that there are many other unsung heroic women who also deserve to be celebrated. I have also tried to include many women of African descent from countries other than the United States. As I was growing up, I learned very little about Black people in other countries—I had no sense of a worldwide Black community of which I was a part— and I hope that this book will go a small way toward filling in that gap, which I suspect others experienced as well.

In these pages you will meet Yelena Khanga, a Black Russian who leads a jet-set life hosting the most popular television show in Russia and performing with a comedy troupe in Brighton Beach, New York; Ana Quirot, a Cuban runner who overcame life-threatening burns and the loss of her unborn daughter to triumph in the Olympic games; the legendary Queen of Sheba; Toni Stone, one of the few women to play professional baseball; and Lulu White, the diamond-studded madam of Mahogany Hall in Storyville, New Orleans.

The book is organized by field of endeavor rather than chronologically. The first chapter, "African Queens," makes it clear that women's lib began centuries ago on the mother continent. "Slaves Who Refused to Bow" recounts the derring-do of women who overcame the shackles of bondage to make their mark on the world. "Freedom Fighters, Rabble Rousers, and Audacious Advocates" is bursting with women who actively fought or are presently fighting to make the world a better, more just place. Women who have made their mark in the halls of power, whether in the world of politics or of business, are depicted in "Powerful Politicos and Bold Businesswomen." Just to prove that Black women can whip up something in the lab as well as in the kitchen, there is chapter 5, "Successful Scientists." "Stars on Track, Field, and Court" displays the talents of Black women athletes. "Sassy Songbirds, Dazzling Dancers, and Talented Thespians," along with chapters 8 and 9, "Artists with Attitude" and "Wonderful Wordsmiths," showcases women who have succeeded in all areas of the arts. Last, but very enjoyably not least, is "Gender Benders, Fabulous Firsts, and Other Outrageous Ladies," full of

women who have done the unusual—or the usual in a very unusual way.

I hope that you will learn something new in these pages and
enjoy yourself along the way, just as I did on my own journey exploring and coming to know these remarkable women.

MAPS

CARIBBEAN ISLANDS,
BRAZIL

Cuba

Haiti

Jamaica

Antigua

Dominica

Barbados

Netherland
Antilles

Trinidad

Brazil

EUROPE,
RUSSIA,
CRIMEA,
TURKEY

Denmark

England

Russia

Crimea

France

Switzerland

Italy

Turkey

UNITED STATES,
CANADA,
MEXICO

AFRICAN
QUEENS

TiYE ▲▲▲▲▲▲▲▲▲▲▲▲▲▲▲▲▲▲▲▲▲▲▲▲

Nubian Queen

TIYE WAS DESTINED to become one of the most influential women in Egyptian history. Born in 1415 B.C.E. in Nubia, she would later come to be the queen mother of Egypt and remain in that position for half a century.

By the time of the reign of Amenhotep III in the fourteenth century B.C.E., Egypt had subjugated Nubia, its neighbor to the south. It was a rare period of dependence, for Nubia has managed, despite continuing threats from Egypt, to remain independent for most of its 5,000-year history. The country was finally overrun by Muslim invaders 600 years ago.

In defiance of all custom, Amenhotep III chose to marry Tiye, a commoner from Nubia, partly to solidify his hold over that country but most certainly also for love. It was customary for a

3

pharaoh to marry a daughter of a pharoah, which could mean marrying his own sister or even his daughter in order to keep the royal bloodlines pure. Amenhotep III chose instead to make Tiye the Great Royal Spouse. But his treatment of Tiye revealed more than political motivations. He held her in great esteem, describing her as "the Princess, the most praised, the lady of grace, sweet in her love, who fills the palace with her beauty, the Regent of the North and South, the Great Wife of the King who loves her, the lady of both lands, Tiye. . . ."

He further demonstrated his affection by erecting, in the Nubian city of Sedeinga, a magnificent temple in her honor—the first time in Egyptian history that a queen had received such an accolade. The many gifts he gave her made her a wealthy woman. Although custom dictated that a queen be portrayed in sculpture and paintings as only half the size of her king, Amenhotep III made sure that Tiye was portrayed as an equal.

Early in the marriage, the king followed custom and attended state occasions with his mother, who was in the royal bloodline. But soon Tiye was his companion not only in private but also on public occasions. Only thirteen when she married, Tiye had at least seven children. Her son Akhenaten became pharoah after his father's death.

Throughout her husband's reign, Tiye helped Ahmenhotep III coordinate state policies, a role she continued when her son Akhenaten became pharoah. But Akhenaten was a disappointment to his mother; he was more interested in religious reform than affairs of state—so much so that under his leadership Egypt lost its military edge. Seeing the situation clearly, Tiye filled the vacuum in leadership by acting as her son's secretary of state. Rulers of client states would appeal directly to Tiye for protection from their enemies. When Akhenaten was succeeded by Tutankhamen, Tiye continued to play an influential role in the politics of the country.

Even more important than her wise political influence, Tiye's reign marked a change in the status of women. For the first time a commoner was proclaimed and depicted as the equal of the king.

The QUEEN *of* SHEBA
Woman of Mystery

MANY PEOPLE CONSIDER the origins of the Queen of Sheba to be an unsolvable mystery. Not so in Ethiopia. There it is a certainty that the woman who entranced King Solomon was the Ethiopian queen named Makeda. According to the *Kebra Nagast* ("Glory of the Kings"), a revered Ethiopian history, Queen Makeda was born in 1020 B.C.E. Upon her father's death, she ascended to the throne, and she was reportedly both beautiful and rich.

An Ethiopian merchant prince named Tamrin engaged in trade with King Solomon of Jerusalem; he was impressed with the king's honest and impartial nature. He shared his opinion with Makeda, who was impressed with his description of this just— and rich—man. She determined to travel to Jerusalem to meet

5

him. Tamrin put together a caravan and guided Makeda's entourage on the journey.

In Jerusalem, Makeda was welcomed by Solomon in royal fashion. He supplied her and her entourage with housing in his palace and wined and dined them, paying special attention to the beauteous Makeda. The two royal personages were delighted with each other's company. Solomon even converted her to his religion, Judaism.

After six months, Makeda informed Solomon that, as much as she would love to stay, she had to return to her duties in Sheba. Solomon was reluctant to let her leave and pleaded with her to remain a short while longer. Makeda agreed. During this continued stay she became pregnant with Solomon's child. Finally she insisted that she return to her country, and reluctantly Solomon saw her on her way, giving her many presents and a ring for what he hoped would be a son. Shortly after she returned to Sheba, she did indeed give birth to a son, naming him Ebna Hakim, which means "son of the wise man."

According to the legend, when their son was twenty-two, she sent him to visit his father, as she had promised to do when she left Jerusalem. Solomon reportedly was overjoyed to see his son, especially since his other heir, Rheabom, was reported to be somewhat foolish. Solomon pleaded with Ebna Hakim to stay in Jerusalem and become his successor, but Ebna insisted on returning to Sheba. Solomon reluctantly let him go, sending with him his counselors' sons, who were trained in Hebraic law, to help with the conversion of the people of Sheba to Judaism. Reportedly, these young men stole the Ark of the Covenant from Jerusalem and took it with them to what is now Ethiopia, where the Ethiopians claim it still remains. The missionaries were successful in their work, forming a community of the Falasha (Black Jews) of Ethiopia, who still form a significant part of the population.

Makeda, the Queen of Sheba, continued to rule until 955 B.C.E., when she was succeeded by Ebna Hakim, who took the name Menelik I.

AMiNA

As Capable as a Man

IT IS IMPOSSIBLE to pinpoint the dates of this fierce warrior's birth or death, but it is believed that Amina ruled sometime during the fifteenth or sixteenth century. She came from a lineage of queens, and was herself the queen of Zaria (or Zazzau) in West Africa, one of the seven states that made up Hausaland (now Nigeria). According to several sources, her mother, Bakwa Turunku, succeeded to the throne around 1535, when Amina was a child.

Demonstrating a remarkable independence, Amina never married, although she was wooed lavishly by many suitors. Instead she trained as a warrior and accompanied one of the chiefs, Karama, during his warring raids. Upon the death of her mother (or of Karama; the record is not clear) she assumed the throne and reigned for thirty-four years.

Under her able leadership, Zaria became the most powerful state in Hausaland. Amina eventually extended her holdings to the sea both on the south and the west. She opened new east–west trade routes and took enormous amounts of tribute, including forty eunuchs and 10,000 kola nuts from one of the subjugated rulers, making her the first person in Hausaland to have such luxuries.

Legend has it that she took a new lover in each town she conquered. This may have seemed a great honor to the male flavor of the evening, but his joy was probably lessened considerably the next morning when she had him beheaded on her way out of town to her next conquest.

Ruling ran in Amina's family. The female chain of command continued after her death, when her sister ascended the throne. She is remembered as "Amina, daughter of Nikatau, a woman as capable as a man," high praise indeed for her time.

NZiNGA
▲▲▲▲▲▲▲▲▲▲▲▲▲▲▲▲▲▲▲▲▲▲▲▲
"King" of Ndongo

In 1583, when Nzinga was born in Ndongo (now Angola), the Portuguese were in a bind. They had lost some of their trading posts in West Africa and the Congo, while their colony in the New World, Brazil, was demanding more and more slave labor. They began to look south to Ndongo for fresh slaves. But Nzinga's father, ruler of the Ndongo people, didn't take the stealing of his people lightly. Hostilities broke out between Nzinga's father and the Portuguese and continued for almost 100 years.

Nzinga's childhood was splendid preparation for her later struggle with the Portuguese. She was a bright, alert child, and her father paid special attention to her education, training her in political, military, and religious matters. She is reported to have killed her first enemy when she was only twelve years old. In 1617 her father was overthrown, his subjects having finally tired of his increasingly tyrannical behavior. Her brother succeeded him, continuing the struggle against the Portuguese. When the situation reached a stalemate, the Portuguese governor requested a cease-fire. Nzinga was sent to negotiate.

Apparently, Nzinga knew a lot about first impressions, for she refused to behave like a conquered subject. She arrived with all the pomp and circumstance of a royal procession, preceded by musicians and accompanied by several handmaidens. There was only one chair in the room where the meeting was held—the governor's throne. Instead of sitting on the pillows that were offered to her, which would have denoted her lesser status, she reportedly summoned one of her women servants, had her kneel on her hands and knees, and then used her as a chair.

Her keen intelligence and her immense dignity impressed the Portuguese. One of the methods she used to gain their confidence during the extended negotiations was to accept their religion. She was baptized into the Catholic faith in the cathedral of Luanda, taking the name Dona Ana de Souza, with the governor and his wife acting as godparents.

Finally, with Nzinga's help, an agreement of peace was settled.

However, the Portuguese did not stick to the terms of the agreement. War broke out again, Nzinga's brother was defeated, and in 1623, at the age of forty-one, she became absolute ruler of her country. The Portuguese forced Nzinga and her people east, where she established the kingdom of Matamba. When dissension arose among her subjects about her rule, she quickly moved to consolidate her power, changing the law so that she was no longer called "Queen," but "King." She even had a harem of young men as her "wives." After this she sometimes wore men's clothing, usually when leading her troops in battle, proving that clothes not only make the man, but the woman as well.

She never ceased to oppose Portuguese rule, although in 1659, in the face of their superior weaponry, she signed a treaty with the Portuguese. She was then seventy-five and had been fighting the Portuguese most of her adult life. She died on December 17, 1663, after which the Portuguese were able to rapidly expand their slave trade in the region.

HeLENA AND SAbLA WaNGEL

▲▲

Guardians of Ethiopia

IN THE SIXTEENTH CENTURY, Ethiopia was a Christian country surrounded by Islamic neighbors. One method Ethiopian kings

used to ensure peace with their neighbors was to marry Moslem
princesses. Following this trend, Emperor Baeda Maryam married the daughter of the Muslim king of Doaro. She was baptized into the Christian faith and took the name of Helena. Her wisdom and knowledge of both the Islamic and Christian worlds helped her direct the policies of her adopted country through the reigns of five kings.

When her husband died in 1478, Helena became regent for their young son, ruling during his minority. During her regency she rebuilt many churches and monasteries that had been destroyed in fighting between Christians and Muslims. She continued to play a pivotal role in the government even after her son came of age. When a Portuguese delegation arrived, she realized that they could be valuable allies against Ethiopia's Islamic enemies.

Her son was killed in fighting, and she again became regent, this time for her grandson. This child died a few months later, and Helena's second son became king. Fourteen years later, he died, and once again Helena became regent, this time for his twelve-year-old son, Lebna Dengel. It was during this period that Portugal and Turkey became more intrusive in Ethiopian affairs. The Turks had conquered Egypt and controlled the Indian Ocean, while the Portuguese controlled the Red Sea and the seas off the East African coast.

In 1509 Helena sent a letter to the Portuguese king, requesting an alliance between their sea forces and her army. It took eleven years for her messenger to return, without the desired alliance. In the meantime Lebna Dengel had come of age, and Helena no longer had as much influence. Unfortunately, unlike his father and uncle, he was hasty and foolhardy and did not always listen to her sage advice. Helena died in 1522, by which time Lebna was foolishly ignoring the Moslem threat to his country.

Lebna Dengel was a competent soldier but had no understanding of the Islamic states and their customs, was high-handed with his own nobles, and was guilty of overconfidence, which led to his downfall. Sure of an easy victory, when the Muslims mounted an attack, he engaged them with only half of his army. Instead he was roundly defeated at the battle of Shembera Kure in 1529. Most of the Ethiopian population was forced to convert to Islam, and most of the royal family was killed or captured. Lebna himself became a fugitive. By 1539 he had been forced into his last stronghold, a monastery on a mountaintop that could only be reached in a basket-lift. He died there in 1540, leaving his widow, Sabla Wangel, in charge of his forces as regent for her son, Galawdewos.

Before his death, Lebna had requested aid from the Portuguese. When the Portuguese arrived, led by Christovao da Gama, son of the explorer Vasco da Gama, widow Sabla descended from her mountain stronghold and traveled with the Portuguese military leader to help him rally the Ethiopians. Her presence brought the people out to volunteer or to provide those who did with food and other necessities. She traveled with the forces, tending the wounded during many battles. In 1543, the Muslim forces were routed, although fighting continued for six more years. When Galawdewos was killed, Sabla's other son Minas came to the throne. He reigned for four years with Sabla's sage advice in his ear. Her last achievement before her death was to make sure that her grandson Sartsa Dengel succeeded to the throne. He proved to be a wise choice, successfully defending his kingdom for the thirty-four years of his reign.

DONA BEATRiCE
▲▲▲▲▲▲▲▲▲▲▲▲▲▲▲▲▲▲▲▲▲▲▲▲▲▲▲
Kongo Mystic

TWO HUNDRED YEARS before the birth of Dona Beatrice in approximately 1682, Kongo, which is now northern Angola, was one of the most powerful states on the west coast of Africa. First contact with the Portuguese, starting in 1482, was peaceful. In 1491 the king of Kongo converted to Christianity, and around 1507 his son, Affonso, attempted to convert Kongo to a Christian kingdom. But the peaceful relationship with the Portuguese was fated to end, due to the Portuguese desire for slaves. Affonso made war on his neighbors, taking prisoners of war to supply the Portuguese with slaves. These wars continued after Affonso's death, leading to the death of Affonso's son, Diogo, and the weakening of the kingdom. By the end of the seventeenth century, Kongo was a shadow of its former self, assaulted by external enemies and internal rivalries.

Needless to say, the Kongo people were upset by the deterioration of their country, providing a fertile ground for a Christian religious revival that they hoped would restore the power the country had had before the slave trade. Kimpa Vita, later to be known as Dona Beatrice, was born into these times, into an aristocratic family. Once when she was sick, a vision of Saint Anthony appeared to her in the form of one of her brothers. This was the beginning of her crusade to restore the kingdom to the glory it had experienced under Affonso. She renounced the material world and began to preach the message that the Kongo must be reborn. She hoped to unite the country under a powerful leader and restore it to its former power and glory. She promoted the myth that she had died and been resurrected like Christ. By 1704, at the age of twenty-two, she was a recognized religious and political leader, in residence in the capital city, São Salvador. The lords let her use their capes as tablecloths, and a retinue of women cleared a path for her wherever she went.

Her cult, called Antonianism, was an Africanized Christianity, holding that Kongo was the Holy Land, that Christ had been born in São Salvador, and that the founders of Christianity were African. The Portuguese were, needless to say, opposed to Dona Beatrice's version of Christianity and were determined to destroy her.

She helped to bring about her own downfall when, claiming she was still a virgin, she gave birth to a son. The people's belief in her began to falter, and the king, at the urging of the Portuguese, arrested her shortly after the birth. The king of Kongo tried to send her to the bishop of Angola for trial, but the Portuguese forced him to try her himself. She was sentenced to be burned at the stake. Not content to dispose of her alone, they burned her child along with her.

If the Portuguese had hoped that her death would put an end to what they considered heresy, they were mistaken. Her faithful followers continued to spread Antonianiasm, until the king was forced, two years after her death, to organize an army to suppress the sect. Although temporarily united under Pedro IV, the country ultimately was absorbed into the Portuguese colony of Angola.

NaNDI
▲▲▲▲▲▲▲▲▲▲▲▲▲▲▲▲▲▲▲▲▲▲▲

The Great She Elephant

NANDI WAS THE mother of Shaka, the founder of the great Zulu empire, and the events of their lives give new meaning to the term "dysfunctional family."

She was the orphaned daughter of the chief of the Langeni tribe, neighbors of the Zulu, which at the time numbered perhaps 1,500. The Langenis were closely related to the Zulu, making marriage between the two clans a terrible violation of Zulu custom.

But Nandi was a headstrong and determined woman, definitely not the obedient type. Despite the taboo, she fell in love with the chief of the Zulu, Senzangakhoma, and became pregnant by him. When Nandi's tribe requested that Senzangakhoma send for her, he replied that she was not pregnant but infected with an intestinal beetle often conveniently blamed for menstrual irregularities. That excuse went out the window when son Shaka was born. Nandi's tribe sent word again, and Shaka's father reluctantly sent for Nandi and installed her as his third wife, but he was none too happy about it. Although some of the scandal of the situation

15

was removed after the marriage, both Nandi and her son continued to be stigmatized. They were truly each other's only friend.

Such an inauspicious beginning was a portent of things to come, for Nandi's marriage was definitely not a match made in heaven. After six years of breaking up and making up, Nandi was sent back to her tribe. However, she and her son were even less welcome there. She had disgraced her clan with a relationship within forbidden kinship lines, she had no man to provide for her, and, to top it off, she was a bit of a shrew. There is nothing like a pushy woman to upset some people; when a heavy famine occurred in the area, Nandi was booted out and eventually ended up living with the Mtetwa tribe, where she and her son finally found some acceptance.

When Shaka was twenty-three, he began to serve in the Mtetwa military and built a reputation as a great warrior. After six years, upon his father's death, he was called back to lead the Zulu tribe, and he began to create what became the great Zulu empire. But the years of disgrace and ostracism had twisted Shaka in ways that became fully apparent upon Nandi's death.

Shaka's grief at losing the one person who had always loved him, combined with the loneliness and hatred created in

Nandi

him in his childhood, sent him into spasms of grief. When told of her death, he ordered summary executions and allowed his people to engage in a frenzy of killing. In the short space of the day and a half following Nandi's death, more than 7,000 people died. On the third day after her death, Nandi was buried. Ten of her handmaidens were buried alive with her, their arms and legs broken. Twelve thousand men were assigned to guard the grave for a year. Shaka decreed that for one year, no crops were to be planted, and no milk (a staple of the Zulu diet) was to be consumed. All women who were found to be pregnant during the year were to be killed, along with their husbands. He even had the cows slaughtered so that the calves would understand what it was like to lose a mother.

He eventually wearied of mourning and called off the edicts. But the excessiveness of his grief, combined with mistreatment of his troops, led to his assassination the following year.

YAA ASANTEWA
Warrior Woman

YAA ASANATEA IS one of the few women in the world to have an international war named after her.

In the 1670s, Osei Tutu, the first ruler of the Asante kingdom in what is now Ghana, created a national faith to unify his country, symbolized by the Golden Stool. Myth had it that the stool, made of wood and decorated with gold, appeared out of a cloud of dust, accompanied by thunder and lightning. Each succeeding ruler was said to be "on the stool," although it would have been sacrilegious for anyone to actually sit on it. On ceremonial occasions it was set on a throne of its own at a higher level than that of the ruler himself. British colonists' failure to understand the importance of the stool led to what is known as the Yaa Asantewa war of 1900–1901.

Yaa Asantewa, born sometime between 1840 and 1860, was mother of and adviser to the ruler of Edweso, one of the Asante states. She would probably have never been known outside her own people if it were not for a considerable miscalculation about the stool by the British, with whom the Asante had been in conflict for many years.

In 1894, as part of the conflict, the leader of the Asante nation and Yaa Asantewa's son were exiled by the British to the Seychelles Islands, off the coast of West Africa. The British proceeded to build a fort in Asante territory, thinking that Asante power had been crushed. And for four years this appeared to be the case. However, secretly Yaa Asantewaa had assumed a leadership role among her people, and, using the exile of their leaders and the mistreatment her people received at the hands of the invaders, stirred up hatred of the British. This wasn't a hard task. The British were a bit miffed that they had had to mount an expedition to force the Asante to accept the installation of a British protectorate and in-

THE "NEW FLOWER"
Taitu, the fourth wife of Menelik II, emperor of Ethiopia from 1889 to 1913, persuaded him to build a home near a warm spring and give parcels of land around it to the nobility. She named it Addis Ababa, which means "new flower." It became the capital city in 1887.

18

sisted that the Asante pay the cost of the expedition, levying stiff taxes. The Asante were hard-pressed to pay, as the British had already confiscated the gold mines that had been the kingdom's principle source of revenue.

When their leaders were exiled, the Asante people had hidden the Golden Stool, which was the symbol of their sovereignty. To demonstrate his authority over the country, the British governor demanded that they surrender the stool so that he could sit upon it. This, of course, would have been sacrilege. The chiefs met secretly to discuss their strategy. Seeing that some of them were intimidated by the British, Yaa Asantewa is reported to have said, "I have seen that some of you fear to go forward to fight for our king. If it were in the brave days of old . . . chiefs would not sit down to see their king taken away without firing a shot. No white man could have dared to speak to the chiefs of the Asante in the way the governor spoke to you chiefs this morning. Is it true that the bravery of the Asante is no more? I cannot believe it. . . . If you, the men of Asante, will not go forward, then we will. We the women will. I shall call upon my fellow women. We will fight the white men. We will fight till the last of us falls in the battlefields."

Her speech worked, and the chiefs refused to surrender the stool. The military attaché who had been sent by the governor to find the stool finally became so frustrated that he bound the citizens of one village and beat them. In retaliation, the Asante, under Yaa Asantewa's leadership, surrounded the British fort, holding it under siege. After three months, 1,400 British reinforcements reached the fort. It took them another three months to begin to subdue their opposition. In the face of the superior firepower of the enemy, the Asante retreated but fought on. Finally only Yaa Asantewa and a few of her troops remained uncaptured. She attempted to negotiate, but her envoys were badly treated by the British and she continued to resist.

The final battle began on September 30, 1900. Most of her troops had been defeated, but Yaa Asantewa continued to elude her pursuers. When she finally was captured she is reported to have spat in her captor's face. It had taken almost 2,000 troops to snare this one woman.

She was exiled to the Seychelles, where she was reunited with her son, and lived there until her death twenty years later. She is still revered among the Asante as "Yaa Asantewa, the warrior woman who carries a gun and a sword of state in battle."

SLAVES
WHO REFUSED TO BOW

CLARA BROWN

▲▲▲▲▲▲▲▲▲▲▲▲▲▲▲▲▲▲▲▲▲▲▲▲▲▲▲▲▲▲▲

Colorado Pioneer

C LARA BROWN, reportedly the first Black woman to cross the plains during the Gold Rush, was born into slavery in 1800 in the state of Virginia. At the age of nine, she and her mother were sent to Kentucky. When she was eighteen, Clara was allowed to marry and had three children. At age thirty-five she was sold by her master and separated from her husband and children. Twenty years later, when she was fifty-five, her third master died, and she was able to buy her freedom. Under Kentucky law this meant she had to leave the state immediately or be subject to re-enslavement.

Clara went to St. Louis and then on to Denver, working as a cook on a wagon train to pay her way on the eight-week journey. She stayed in Denver long enough to help two ministers start a Sunday school and then moved to Central City, Colorado. She

23

established the first laundry in Central City and did some nursing. A devout woman, she also organized a Sunday school and a church and became the first female member of the Colorado Society of Pioneers.

She was smart enough to invest in mining claims, some of which paid off, and by the mid-1860s she was worth approximately $10,000. She now had the funds, at the age of sixty-six, to begin to look for her family, an intention she had carried with her ever since they were separated. She searched the Reconstruction South for her husband and children, to no avail. Although unable to find her own family, she helped many others do so; she returned to Colorado with sixteen men and women who had been freed by the Civil War and helped them get established. She also financed several wagon trains of African Americans from the South who traveled west in search of better lives.

Clara Brown

A woman with a big heart despite her personal losses, she became known for her charity, and she never turned away anyone in need. Late in her life, probably after she had given up all hope, she was reunited with her daughter and a granddaughter. When she died at age eighty-two, she was buried with honors by the Colorado

Pioneers Association. A plaque was placed in the St. James Methodist Church to denote her role as one of its founders and a chair in the Opera House was named in her honor.

BidDY MASON

▲▲▲▲▲▲▲▲▲▲▲▲▲▲▲▲▲▲▲▲▲▲▲▲▲▲▲▲

Walking Into History

IT'S EASY ENOUGH to get to California from Mississippi these days. One can fly, drive, or take a train. Biddy Mason walked. Born in 1818, Mason spent her childhood on a plantation in Mississippi, assisting the house servants and midwives in the household. In 1836, she was given to her owner's cousin, Rebecca Smith, as a wedding present. Mason managed the affairs of the Smith's plantation and helped care for the sickly Rebecca. Rebecca's husband, Robert Smith, fathered Mason's three children, not an unusual occurrence in the antebellum South.

Robert Smith became a Mormon, converted by Elder John Brown, and in 1848 the Smith household, including Mason and forty other slaves, became part of the Mormon migration westward. Mason walked almost the entire distance from Mississippi to Utah. The slaves had been promised their freedom if they accompanied the family on its journey, a promise Smith promptly broke.

The Smiths and their slaves stayed in Utah for three years. Then Brigham Young called for volunteers to help create a settlement in

Southern California, and the Smiths signed up. Again, Mason accompanied the family. Once there, Mason met people from the Black community in Los Angeles. In 1855, Robert Smith planned to move to Texas. But California was a free state, and Mason boldly petitioned for her freedom. The judge who heard the petition placed Mason and her three children in protective custody, to make sure no attempts were made to spirit them away before his ruling was made. On January 21, 1856, Biddy Mason, her three daughters, and ten other slaves belonging to Robert Smith were emancipated, a precedent-setting event for Black settlers in the West.

Settling into life in Los Angeles, she became a nurse and midwife, traveling as far as San Diego and Santa Barbara to assist her clients and taking care of the sick in hospitals and jails. She also invested in real estate, establishing a base for a family fortune that made her son the richest Black man in Los Angeles at the turn of the century. A founding member of the First African Methodist Episcopal Church in Los Angeles, she also founded a day care center to take care of Black children.

Mason died on January 15, 1891, having served the Black community of Southern California for forty years. Her gravesite remained unmarked until March 1988 when Los Angeles Mayor Tom Bradley presided over a ceremony installing a tombstone erected by the First African Methodist Episcopal Church. November 16, 1989 was proclaimed Biddy Mason Day in Los Angeles, and an 8-by-81-foot timeline memorial wall was unveiled at the Broadway Spring Center in a ceremony attended by two of Mason's great granddaughters.

SUSiE KING TAYLoR

Civil War Nurse

SUSIE TAYLOR was the only Black woman to write about her participation in the Civil War, describing her adventures as laundress, teacher, and nurse.

Although she was the daughter of a domestic slave, when she was a youngster she lived in freedom with her grandmother in Savannah, where her grandmother made a living bartering chickens. In Savannah, Susie met two white children who taught her to read and write, even though it was against the law to do so.

When the Civil War began, Susie went to the Sea Islands off the coast of South Carolina with an uncle and his family; here, she was recruited by the Union Army to teach freed slaves, both children and adults. Later she worked both as a laundress and nurse for the Union forces without compensation, learning how to shoot a rifle as well as care for the sick and dying. She worked with Clara Barton while Barton was in the Sea Islands. Susie remained with her regiment until the fall of Charleston in February 1865.

> God is just; when he created man he made him in his image, and never intended one should misuse the other. All men are born free and equal in his sight.
>
> —Susie King Taylor

After the war, she and her husband settled in Savannah and opened a school. Her husband died in 1866 and she moved to the Georgia countryside. Unfulfilled by country life, she returned to Savannah, where she opened a night school for freedmen and taught until 1872. Teaching paid so little that she took a position as a laundress and cook for a wealthy white family in Savannah. The family often journeyed to New England during the summer, and Susie would accompany them. She eventually decided to move to Boston, where she married again and became involved in civic activities, such as organizing the Women's Auxiliary Corps of the Grand Army of the Republic. In 1902, ten years before her death, she wrote her memoirs, *Reminiscences of My Life in Camp with the 33rd United States Colored Troops Late 1st SC Volunteers.*

She ventured south again in 1898, when her son was dying, and found that although the institution of slavery was officially dead, it had transformed into a comparable form of oppression under the Jim Crow laws. She never went south again.

MaRY ELLEN PLEASaNT

▲▲▲▲▲▲▲▲▲▲▲▲▲▲▲▲▲▲▲▲▲▲▲▲▲▲▲▲▲▲

The Black City Hall

MARY ELLEN PLEASANT was a legend in her own time, so it's difficult to sort out fact from fiction in her history. She told various versions of her life story herself, and later historians have often repeated the half-truths and lies that were spread about her by the journalists of her time.

There are stories that she was a slave from Georgia or Virginia, but Pleasant herself claimed to have been born in Philadelphia in

1814 to a free woman and a wealthy white planter. Either way, she ended up in Massachusetts, indentured to a Quaker merchant in Nantucket. Her service ended in 1841, and she became a tailor's assistant.

She married a man named Smith and the couple worked on the Underground Railroad, helping escaped slaves from the South flee to the northern states or to Canada. When her husband died, she inherited quite a bit of money, which he wanted her to use for abolitionist causes.

She remarried to a man named Pleasant and was soon forced to flee New England. The Fugitive Slave Law passed in 1850, which allowed slave hunters to seize runaways anywhere and return them to their masters, made her life in the North precarious. Her husband went to San Francisco, looking for a safer place, and she joined him there in 1852. In the late 1850s, she reportedly went to Canada, where she aided John Brown, the militant abolitionist who was planning the raid on Harper's Ferry, by giving him money to buy land in Canada for the slaves he planned to free. Brown's mission was a failure. He was hanged, and Mary barely escaped with her life.

She returned to San Francisco, becoming an entrepreneur and investor. One of her restaurants was the meeting place for some of the city's most influential and wealthy people who developed a high regard for her. She used her influence with them to obtain jobs and privileges for the Black citizens of San Francisco, thus

> You tell those newspaper people that they may be smart, but I'm smarter. They deal with words. Some folks say that words were made to reveal thought. That ain't so. Words were made to conceal thought.
> —Mary Ellen Pleasant

earning her restaurant the nickname of "The Black City Hall." She was so successful in her ventures that she was soon advising her investors on their own financial affairs.

This feisty female continued her activism in other ways. She harbored fugitive slaves, which was illegal, and supported the passage of the 1863 California law that gave Black Americans the right to testify in court. In 1868 she filed a discrimination lawsuit, the first of its kind, against the North Beach Railroad Company because she had not been allowed to board a streetcar. She was awarded $500 in damages.

Pleasant was one of the most talked-about women in the San Francisco press. More than 100 articles were published about her, many of them unfavorable and libelous. She was called a voodoo queen and a madam, among other things. It was hard for many people to believe that a Black woman could have achieved such success in life without treachery or magic powers. Despite the defamation of her good name, she continued her work for her people until her death in 1904.

ELLEN CRAfT

Escaping in Drag

DETERMINED TO BE FREE, Ellen Craft staged one of the most unique escapes in slave history. She was born in Clinton, Georgia, in 1826. Her mother was a household slave and her father was her

Elizabeth Freeman and her sisters were slaves in the Massachusetts home of Colonel John Ashley. The Declaration of Independence had been written in 1776, and everyone was talking about freedom, liberty, and equality. Elizabeth listened to these discussions while she served meals. When the Revolutionary War ended in 1781, Elizabeth decided it was time to do something about her own liberty. She left the Ashley household and refused to return. A young lawyer, Theodore Sedgwick, agreed to represent her, arguing that according to the Declaration of Independence and the Massachusetts Constitution adopted in 1780, she should be freed. Her case was heard in 1781 and the jury agreed. In addition, the judge ordered Colonel Ashley to pay Elizabeth 30 shillings in damages. After her victory, she went to work for her lawyer's family. Her court case effectively ended slavery in the state of Massachusetts.

mother's master, Major James Smith. The major's wife was not pleased with Ellen's presence, a constant reminder of her husband's infidelity, and retaliated by giving the eleven-year-old Ellen to her daughter Eliza, who lived in Macon, Georgia. In 1846 Ellen married a fellow slave. Two years later they decided they'd had enough of slavery.

Ellen, who could pass for white, disguised herself as a slave master traveling to Philadelphia, with her husband William acting as her valet. Arriving safely in Boston, the couple settled down and Ellen made a living as a seamstress. Two years later, in 1850, their freedom was threatened by the Fugitive Slave Act. Ellen's owner doggedly tracked her down and sent slave hunters to bring her back.

Returning to slavery was not an option for Ellen and William. They fled to England, where they remained for nineteen years, settling in Hammersmith, London. Ellen continued to work as a seamstress and also spoke on the antislavery lecture circuit. Both she and William served as members of the executive committee of the London Emancipation Committee.

After the Civil War, they returned to the United States, and in 1871 they bought property in Ways Station, Georgia, where they grew cotton and rice. Ellen also started a school for local children. They were unable to make a financial go of it and were forced to leave Georgia, returning to Charleston, South Carolina, where they finished out their days with Ellen's family.

AMANdA BERRY SMiTh

The Singing Pilgrim

AMANDA BERRY SMITH was one of the most famous Black women of her day. Her father bought his family's freedom when she was a toddler, and by 1850 they had moved from Long Green, Maryland, to York County in southeastern Pennsylvania. Despite living in the North, she learned to read and write at home because Black children were not allowed to attend the local schools.

At thirteen she went to work as a domestic, and married at seventeen. By the time of the Civil War, she had separated from her husband and moved to Philadelphia, where she met and married a deacon of the African Methodist Episcopal Church who was twenty years her senior. They moved to Greenwich Village in New York City, where Amanda took in laundry to supplement the family income.

During this time her religious faith deepened and in 1869, after her husband's death from cancer, she began to conduct revivals at African Methodist Episcopal churches in New Jersey and New York, later speaking at white Methodist churches as well. Thus began a missionary career that lasted forty-five years and covered four continents.

As her fame grew, newspapers of the time called her "the singing pilgrim." In 1872 she attended the first AME church general conference and in 1875 she became a charter member of the Women's Christian Temperance Union. The WCTU national secretary invited Amanda to accompany her to England for temperance revivals. She left in 1878 and spent twelve years in England, Scotland, India, and West Africa, working for education and temperance reform.

Amanda returned to the United States suffering from debilitating arthritis and malaria, but she continued her missionary work. She conducted revival meetings, wrote an autobiography, and testified before Congress about the liquor traffic. In 1893, she settled in Chicago, where she raised funds to open an orphan home and an industrial school for Black children in Harvey, Illinois, a temperance settlement outside of Chicago.

The school opened in 1899 in a building she had purchased. She later bought the adjoining eighteen lots. She operated the orphan home without any government funds, and raising money was a continual struggle. She continued to raise funds for the school until she was forced to retire in 1913 because of her failing health.

George Sebring, a wealthy Ohio businessman and longtime supporter of hers, offered Amanda a cottage in the town he had established in Florida and which was named after him. She suffered a series of strokes there and died on February 24, 1915.

ELiZABETH KECkLEY

▲▲▲▲▲▲▲▲▲▲▲▲▲▲▲▲▲▲▲▲▲▲▲▲▲▲▲▲▲

Pioneering Gossip Writer

ELIZABETH KECKLEY'S early life reads like the typical slave woman's story. She lived on a plantation with her mother in Hillsborough, North Carolina. Her father lived on another plantation 100 miles away; she saw him only at Easter and Christmas until she was seven or eight. Then his master moved away, taking her father along, and she and her mother never saw him again, although they kept in touch through letters for many years. When she was a teenager, her master gave her to his son and his bride as a wedding present. As so often happened to slave women, a friend of her master forced himself on her, and she had a son. Her master had promised her that on his death she could buy freedom for herself and her son, but when the time came she did not have the money.

Still a slave, she was moved to St. Louis, where she began to use the dressmaker skills she had learned from her mother. By 1855 she had enough money to buy freedom for both herself and her son. She moved to Baltimore, where she started a school for Black girls, teaching sewing and etiquette. From there she moved to Washington, D.C., where she came to the attention of First Lady Mary Todd Lincoln. Elizabeth became Mary's dressmaker and eventually her close friend. She was one of the few people who could tolerate Mary's sharp tongue and unstable personality. The friendship was put to the test and lost when Elizabeth printed *Behind the Scenes: Thirty Years a Slave and Four Years in the White House,* a book that included many details about life in the White House.

Mary Todd Lincoln had been criticized for years for her love of expensive clothes, furs, and jewelry. She was called pretentious and extravagant, criticisms that increased after her husband's death. Elizabeth, one of Mary's closest friends, knew she was impulsive, ambitious, and insecure, but she also knew that she was loving and charitable. She wrote *Behind the Scenes* intending to support her friend and help set the record straight, but her perceived betrayal of confidences created an irreparable rift in the relationship.

Elizabeth continued her career in Washington for some years, then moved to Xenia, Ohio, in 1892, where she joined the faculty of Wilberforce University as a sewing instructor. She represented

Elizabeth Keckley

Wilberforce at the 1893 Columbian World's Exhibition in Chicago and then returned to Washington, D.C., where she continued sewing until her eyesight failed. She finished out her life at the Home for Destitute Women and Children, which she had helped to establish.

MARY BoWSER

Union Spy

MARY BOWSER was born on the Van Lew plantation near Richmond, Virginia. John Van Lew died in 1851, and the women of the family, abolitionists all, promptly freed his slaves, probably setting John spinning in his grave. Mary continued to work for the Van Lew family as a servant for a while, and then the family sent her to Philadelphia for an education. She was living there when the Civil War broke out.

Daughter Elizabeth Van Lew was a Union sympathizer and became one of the most famous Union spies. Feigning feeblemindedness as she nursed Union soldiers held in Libby Prison in Richmond, Virginia, earned her the nickname Crazy Bet. She helped the soldiers escape, hiding them in her home, where they would pass her all the information they gained listening to their Confederate guards. Elizabeth then sent the information through the lines in coded messages.

Deciding she needed to infiltrate Confederate president Jefferson Davis' own home, Elizabeth sent for Mary in Philadelphia and obtained a position for her as a servant in the Confederate White House. Copying her former mistress' technique, Mary feigned feeblemindedness so well that the Davises and their guests spoke freely in front of her. She also managed to read Confederate dispatches while she cleaned and dusted Davis' office. She memorized all the information she heard and read and would recite it each night to Elizabeth, who translated it into code. Mary and Crazy Bet's joint efforts enabled General Grant and the Union Army to outmaneuver the Rebels and contributed to the fall of Richmond in 1864.

Mary kept a diary of her spy work, which is reputed to be fascinating, but it is owned by a Richmond family who have never allowed it to be made available to the public.

HARRiET JACOBS
▲▲▲▲▲▲▲▲▲▲▲▲▲▲▲▲▲▲▲▲

Extraordinary Author

HARRIET JACOBS withstood an early life of abuse to go on to author the most important slave narrative ever written by an African American woman. Born into slavery in North Carolina in 1813, she was six years old when her mother died; her mistress brought the girl into her home and taught her to read and to sew. When

Harriet was twelve years old, her kindly mistress died, and she was inherited by the mistress' three-year-old niece. Her life instantly took a turn for the worse. Her young mistress' father sexually abused Harriet and threatened to make her his concubine. To avoid that, Harriet began a relationship with a neighbor, a white attorney, and bore him two children. But her master continued his sexual demands and threatened to send her and her children to a plantation. Knowing that if they became plantation slaves they would probably never be able to attain their freedom, Harriet and her children ran away.

The children's father bought their freedom, and the three stayed with Harriet's grandmother, a freed slave who lived in Edenten, North Carolina. Her master's intense search for Harriet prevented her from leaving Edenton. Various sympathetic neighbors, Black and white, hid her until her grandmother and uncle built a hiding place for her in a crawlspace above their porch. She hid in that tiny space—7 feet by 9 feet by 3 feet high—for seven years. Her children were sent north, and finally, in 1842, Harriet escaped and joined them.

She found work as a domestic in New York City, then moved to Rochester in 1849, where she joined her brother, who had also escaped slavery. He had become an antislavery lecturer and activist, and through him, Harriet became part of an abolitionist group. Together they ran an antislavery reading room. She moved back to New York City, where her master tracked her down and tried to capture her and her children. Harriet was determined to remain free, and was equally determined not to acknowledge the slave system by purchasing her freedom, so she fled to Massachusetts.

Against her wishes, a friend purchased her freedom and that of her children, ending her need to run.

A few years earlier, she had told a friend, Amy Post, a Quaker abolitionist, about her history and the sexual abuse common to Black women slaves. Amy urged her to write her story. It took her five years to complete the manuscript and she spent several more trying to find a publisher, both in the United States and in England. Finally, in 1861, she published it herself under the title *Incidents in the Life of a Slave Girl Written by Herself,* using the pseudonym Linda Brent. (For many years the book was thought to be a novel written by a white woman. It wasn't until 1987 and the release of an annotated edition that Harriet was established as the author.)

With the book's publication, Harriet became a minor celebrity among abolitionist women. Within months of its release, the Civil War had begun and Harriet was determined to help. Using her newfound fame, she raised money and supplies to help Black refugees. She and her daughter Louisa went to Alexandria, Virginia, where they provided emergency health care and established the Jacobs Free School for the children of refugees.

> You never knew what it is to be a slave; to be entirely unprotected by law or custom; to have the laws reduce you to the condition of a chattel, entirely subject to the will of another. You never exhausted your ingenuity in avoiding the snares, and eluding the power of a hated tyrant; you never shuddered at the sound of his footsteps, and trembled within hearing of his voice.
> **—Harriet Jacobs**

In 1865, Harriet and Louisa took their relief efforts to Savannah. Understanding the connections between racism and sexism, Louisa joined Susan B. Anthony in a fight to win the right to vote for women and African Americans in New York state.

Harriet and Louisa went to London in 1868 to raise money for an orphanage and old folks' home for Black citizens of Savannah, but it was never built. Escalating Ku Klux Klan violence made it inadvisable to remain in Georgia. Harriet and her daughter returned to Massachusetts, eventually settling in Cambridge, where Harriet ran a boardinghouse. The two later moved to Washington, D.C., where they continued to help freed Blacks. They never again returned south. Harriet died in Washington in 1897 and was buried in Cambridge.

FREEDOM FIGHTERS,

RABBLE ROUSERS,
AND AUDACIOUS ADVOCATES

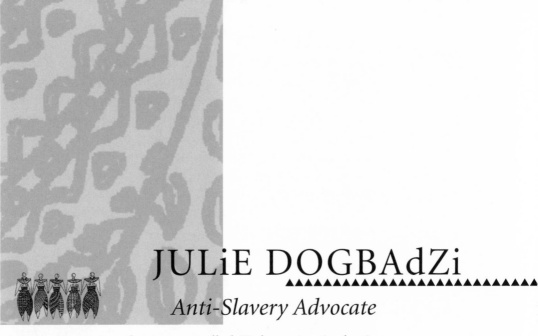

JULiE DOGBAdZi

▲▲▲▲▲▲▲▲▲▲▲▲▲▲▲▲▲▲▲▲▲▲▲▲

Anti-Slavery Advocate

I N ACCORDANCE WITH the custom called *Trokose,* practiced primarily in the Volta region of Ghana even today, a young girl can be enslaved to a shrine to atone for an offense by a member of her family. That's what happened to Julie Dogbadzi. When she was seven years old, in 1981, she was given into slavery by her family because of a theft committed by her grandfather. If she could not work or refused sex with the priest, she was beaten. During the fourteen years she was enslaved, she had two children.

Several times she tried unsuccessfully to escape. Finally, in 1995, she managed to flee with her children to a town sixty miles away and discovered International Needs Ghana, a nonprofit organization that has helped free 1,600 Trokosi slaves and return them to normal lives. They gave her training as a baker so that she could support herself and her children. She now works for International Needs helping to liberate other women and was part of a successful campaign for legislation in Ghana outlawing slavery. There are still an estimated 4,000 women enslaved at these shrines, although the government claims that there is now no slavery in Ghana and no women in any shrines. Julie continues to speak out to government officials and journalists. In 1999, out of 100,000 applicants worldwide, she was awarded the 1999 Reebok Human Rights Award.

FLO KeNNEdY

▲▲▲▲▲▲▲▲▲▲▲▲▲▲▲▲▲▲▲▲▲▲▲

The Mouth That Roared

FLO KENNEDY is one of the most effective activists that civil rights, feminism, and gay rights has ever had. Flornyce Rae Kennedy was born in 1916 in Kansas City, Missouri, to protective and loving parents. After Flo graduated from high school, she worked in various jobs until 1942, when her mother died and Flo moved to New York City.

In 1944 she began pre-law courses at Columbia University. Her application to Columbia Law School was initially rejected, but Flo was not one to sit idly by and let that happen. She paid the

dean an impassioned visit, and her acceptance into law school
followed. She graduated in 1951, working as a law clerk until she
opened her own law office. As a Black woman lawyer in the '50s,
she had difficulty earning a living, so much so that one Christmas
she worked at Bloomingdale's to pay
the rent for her office. The early 1960s
saw the beginning of her political involvement when she began to doubt
the ability of the law to change social
conditions. In 1966 she created the
Media Workshop, which fought discrimination in and through the
media.

FLO-ISMS

"Every form of bigotry can be found in ample supply in the legal system of our country."

"Unity in a movement situation is over-rated. If you were the Establishment, which would you rather see coming in the door, 500 mice or one lion?"

"The biggest sin is sitting on your ass."

"There are very few jobs that actually require a penis or vagina. All other jobs should be open to everybody."

"If men could get pregnant, abortion would be a sacrament."

Flo was not a timid soul. Politeness
was not her middle name. She soon
developed a reputation for being loud,
foul-mouthed, and rude—but effective. The result of an outburst at an
antiwar convention in Montreal was
an invitation to speak in Washington,
marking the beginning of her speak-
ing career. For decades, she spoke out on behalf of civil rights,
women's rights, and gay rights. She also advocated for prostitutes
and the poor. During the 1970s she frequently teamed up for
speaking engagements with Gloria Steinem. When Shirley
Chisholm ran for president, she formed the Feminist Party to
support her.

SEPTiMA CLARk

▲▲▲▲▲▲▲▲▲▲▲▲▲▲▲▲▲▲▲▲▲▲▲▲▲▲▲▲▲▲▲▲

Pioneering Civil Rights Worker

SEPTIMA CLARK's father had been a slave. Her mother was born free in Charleston and had spent her early childhood in Haiti. Clark's mother was dignified and assertive, her father gentle and nonviolent, all traits that Septima inherited. They stood her in good stead later on in life as a crusader for Black education in the United States.

A love of learning ran in the family and in 1916, at the age of eighteen, Clark graduated from a private school for Black teachers and passed the state exam to teach in rural areas. Blacks were not allowed to teach in Charleston proper, so for three years she taught on John's Island, South Carolina. Conditions there were difficult for Black workers. While mothers worked in the fields, they would place their babies in boxes at the ends of the rows, where the children were bitten by flies and mosquitoes, subjecting them to malaria. Many children did not live past the age of two. Clark tried to improve health conditions and conducted workshops on health issues for the workers.

The school itself was a primitive log cabin. The children often had to use the floor as a desk. The Black teachers were paid less than half the salary of the white teachers, a situation Clark was not willing to quietly accept. She joined the fight for equal pay for Black teachers and for Black teachers to be able to work in the

Charleston schools. While she was on John's Island, she joined the NAACP and became known as an equal rights advocate.

In 1920 she married a sailor she met in Charleston and had two children. Sadly her daughter died soon after birth, and her husband died of kidney failure after only five years of marriage. Because she was having trouble providing for him, when her son was ten she sent him to live with her in-laws. She continued to further her education, studying with W. E. B. Du Bois at Atlanta University and strengthening her commitment to social justice. In 1947 she returned to Charleston to care for her mother, who had had a stroke. She taught school while continuing her civil rights activities and became membership chairperson for the local NAACP chapter.

In 1956, the South Carolina legislature passed a law forbidding city employees to belong to civil rights organizations. Clark was fired for refusing to resign from the NAACP, losing her retirement benefits just four years short of retirement. It took twenty years for her finally to win reinstatement of those benefits.

Unable to find work in South Carolina, she went to work for the Highlander Folk School in Monteagle, Tennessee. Highlander was one of the citizenship schools that had sprung up across the South in the '50s, serving as planning centers for Black and white community activists, providing people with literacy training, and empowering them to vote. She spent five years there, once conducting a workshop on the United Nations that was attended by Rosa Parks.

I have a great belief in the fact that whenever there is chaos, it creates wonderful thinking. I consider chaos a gift.
—**Septima Clark**

Highlander closed in 1961. At the age of sixty-three, Clark became director of education for the Southern Christian Leadership Conference (SCLC), traveling across the South visiting citizenship schools.

In 1970 she retired from active work with the SCLC, but she was not one to rest on her laurels. She began working for the American Field Service and organized day care facilities. When she was seventy-eight she served two terms on the Charleston School Board. For her many accomplishments she received a host of awards, including an Honorary Doctorate of Human Letters from the College of Charleston, a Living Legacy Award presented by President Jimmy Carter, and the Order of the Palmetto from the state of South Carolina. She died in her hometown of Charleston on December 15, 1987.

LUCY PARSoNS

Black Anarchist

LUCY PARSONS was the first prominent Black female American leftist. Born in Waco, Texas, in 1853, she met and married a former Confederate Army scout turned radical. Their mixed marriage forced them to leave Texas in a hurry, and in 1873 they ended up in Chicago, where they both joined the Workingmen's Party, a socialist organization. Three years later, Lucy was writing articles for the *Socialist* and speaking on behalf of the Working Women's

Union. Besides writing in support of socialist causes, she wrote eloquently against lynchings and racist violence in the South. In true socialist form, she viewed racism as primarily a class question. She soon leaned even farther left, becoming an anarchist, advocating abolition of the state and free exchange of products without profit.

> Are there any so stupid as to believe these outrages have been. . . heaped upon the Negro because he is Black? Not at all. It is because he is poor. It is because he is dependent. Because he is poorer as a class than his white wage-slave brother of the North.
>
> **—Lucy Parsons**

In 1883, she helped found the International Working People's Association. By 1884 she was urging the jobless to "learn to use explosives." She was one of the organizers of the general strike of May 1, 1886, in which workers were demanding an eight-hour workday. On the third day of demonstrations in Haymarket Square, a bomb was thrown at police. Her husband and eight other IWPA members were arrested for the crime, although proof was sketchy at best. Lucy and others worked tirelessly to free them, but her husband, along with three other defendants, was executed in 1887.

Lucy's faith in anarchist and socialist causes never faltered. She continued to lecture at radical gatherings in the United States and England. In 1891 she began publishing a newspaper called *Freedom: A Revolutionary Anarchist-Communist Monthly,* writing articles about women's issues: rape, divorce, women's oppression. She believed that the establishment of a socialist society would erase the evils of racism and sexism.

She was one of only two women who attended the founding convention of the Industrial Workers of the World (IWW) in 1905.

She led mass demonstrations of the homeless and unemployed in San Francisco and Chicago in 1914 and 1915 respectively, and vigorously opposed World War I. In 1927 she joined the International Labor Defense, a communist-led organization working to defend "class war prisoners," including African Americans unjustly accused of crimes. She joined the Communist Party in 1939, remaining a member until she lost her life three years later in a house fire.

CLAUdiA JoNES

▲▲▲▲▲▲▲▲▲▲▲▲▲▲▲▲▲▲▲

Caring Communist

CLAUDIA JONES was one of the few Black women to rise to a prominent position in the Communist Party of the United States. She was born in Port of Spain, British West Indies (now Trinidad) in 1924 and moved with her family to Harlem when she was nine. Although she showed promise as a journalist when she was a teenager, she was forced to drop out of school during the Depression to work. Her attention was drawn to the Communist Party by the efforts of the International Labor Defense campaign to free the "Scottsboro boys"—nine young men falsely accused of raping two white women and sentenced to death—and at eighteen she joined the Young Communist League, rising through the ranks quickly to become national director of the YCL. Although she was known for her work for civil rights, during World War II she became a leading party spokesperson for women's rights. After the war she was appointed to the party's women's commission, and for a while was secretary of that organization.

During the late 1940s she was arrested several times, and the United States government attempted to deport her. In 1951 she was indicted for violating the Smith Act and imprisoned in Alderson Federal Reformatory for Women. She became a symbol for radical Black women, who marched and petitioned for her release. She was forced to complete her one-year sentence even though she was in poor health.

In December 1955 she was deported to London, where she continued to fight for civil and women's rights. She was founder and editor of the left-wing *West Indian Gazette* in the late 1950s, and in 1962 was a guest editor of *Soviet Women*. She died Christmas Day, 1965, due to the tuberculosis she had contracted as a teenager and which was worsened by her stay in prison. She is buried in London next to Karl Marx.

LOUiSE PATTERSoN
Leader of the Left

LOUiSE PATTERSON was one of the few Black women leaders of the activist Left for more than seventy years. She was born in Chicago in 1901 but grew up in various towns in the West, places where African Americans were not always welcome. When she was eighteen her family settled in Oakland, California.

She was one of the first African American women to graduate from the University of California at Berkeley, with the added distinction of graduating cum laude. She went to the University of Chicago for graduate studies, but left before they were complete. She then taught grade school in Pine Bluff, Arkansas, before teaching business administration at Hampton Institute in Virginia. After a year she was forced to resign because, in a portent of her growing activism, she had backed the students during a student strike.

She received a scholarship from the National Urban League, which allowed her to move to New York City to study social work at the New School. She became a member of the Congregational Educational Society, which worked on race and labor issues. There she met and married Wallace Thurman, a leading figure in the Harlem Renaissance, but the union was short-lived. She worked for Zora Neale Hurston and Langston Hughes as a secretary when they were collaborating on the play *Mule Bone*.

During this time, like many other Black Americans, she became fascinated with the Soviet Union, which promised a classless society with no racial prejudice. This sounded like a dream come true for Black people from the United States. She and sculptor Augusta Savage formed the Vanguard Club for Harlem artists. Some of the members of the Vanguard formed a branch of the Friends of the Soviet Union, of which Louise became secretary. A leading member of the Communist Party USA asked her to head up a special mission to the Soviet Union, a task she gladly accepted. In June 1932 she led a group of African Americans, including Dorothy West and Langston Hughes, to the Soviet Union for the purpose of making a film about the exploitation of Black people in the United States. Wherever they went in the Soviet Union, they were treated like celebrities. The film was eventually cancelled, but the trip was always a highlight of her life.

After she returned to the United States she went to work for the National Committee for the Defense of Political Prisoners. Through her work there she met William Patterson, a member of the Communist Party and one of the lawyers for the Scotsboro boys. William and Louise married in 1940. Their marriage lasted until Williams' death in 1980.

Louise Patterson worked tirelessly against injustice with many leftist organizations, such as the International Workers Order and the Civil Rights Congress. She was a founding member of the Sojourners for Truth and Justice, along with women such as Shirley Graham Du Bois, Alice Childress, and Charlotta Spears Bass. The Sojourners, in the midst of the McCarthy era, aided embattled African American men, including Paul Robeson, with whom she and her husband were close friends. Louise helped organize construction workers in Louisiana and fought on behalf of political prisoners everywhere. She was at the Peekskill incident, when people attending a Robeson concert were attacked while state troopers stood by and did nothing, and she was later arrested by Birmingham Police Commissioner Eugene "Bull" Connor while on a civil rights organizing trip in Alabama.

In 1982 she returned to the San Francisco Bay Area to live with her daughter. She was known for bringing people together for stimulating conversation. Jessica Mitford, Beah Richards, Maya

Angelou, Ruby Dee, and Ossie Davis were frequent visitors to her home. In recognition of her lifelong activism, in 1991 she was given the Fannie Lou Hamer Award by the University of California at Berkeley Department of African American Studies. She died in 1999.

AUtHERiNE LUCY FoSTER

Integrating Education

AUTHERiNE FOSTER, a pioneer of integrated southern schools, is famous for being willing to take risks for her education. She was one of ten children in a farming family. When she wasn't in school, she helped work in the fields, picking cotton, and raising watermelon, sweet potatoes, and peanuts. She graduated from high school in 1947 and went to Selma University in Selma, Alabama, and Miles College in Fairfield, Alabama, where she met Hugh Foster, her future husband.

She graduated from Miles with a B.A. in English in 1952 and then made the decision that changed her life: she decided to go to graduate school at the University of Alabama. Having grown up in the segregated South, she knew she was in for a fight. She asked the NAACP to assist her, and several attorneys, including Thurgood Marshall, were assigned to her case. While they laid the legal foundation, she worked at various jobs. The case went to court in

July 1953; two years later, on June 29, 1955, the court issued an
order forcing Lucy to be admitted. On July 1st the order was
amended to include any African American seeking admission.

Autherine enrolled on February 3, 1956, as a graduate student. When she attempted to attend classes on the third day, she was greeted by a mob of students and townspeople who threw eggs at her. Police had to escort her to her classes. That evening the university used the unrest as an excuse to suspend her, saying it was for her safety and that of the other students.

The NAACP promptly filed suit, accusing the administrators of supporting the mob. But they were forced to withdraw those charges because they could not find evidence to support them. The school used the suit as an excuse to expel Autherine. Several European schools invited her to study abroad, but she declined.

She had become too controversial and had difficulty finding a job. In 1956 she moved to Texas, married her college sweetheart, had five children, and eventually found work as a teacher. The Fosters lived in Texas for seventeen years before returning to Alabama in 1974.

In 1988 two professors from the University of Alabama asked Autherine to speak to a class about her experiences. One of the students asked her if she wanted to re-enroll. She said she hadn't thought about it, but would consider it. Several professors began to work to overturn her expulsion, which they accomplished in April 1988. In 1989, at age sixty, Autherine re-entered the University of Alabama, bringing her life full circle. Her daughter enrolled at the same time, and they both received degrees in 1992.

AYSE BiRCaN

▲▲▲▲▲▲▲▲▲▲▲▲▲▲▲▲▲▲▲

Turkish Activist

IN THE LATE nineteenth century, when Ayse Bircan's great-grand-father was seven years old, he was bought by a Turk who had come to Mecca on pilgrimage. Part of the purpose of the Turk's pilgrimage was to buy, free, and adopt a Black slave, a good deed that, according to the Muslim religion, would help pave his way to heaven. Black slaves in the Middle East were not uncommon. Although the Western slave trade is what we hear about most, a sizeable trade in slaves from the east coast of Africa to the Middle East predated the Atlantic slave trade. Although the Turk later had children of his own, he treated this boy as his own son, and when he died his property was divided equally among all his children.

To this day, Ayse's family descended from the great-grandfa-ther and their white relatives still interact and get along well. Her father's family had been the only Black family in his village, and her mother's family had been the only Black family in hers. After a matchmaker told Ayse's mother about her father, she ran away to his village and married him. They moved to Istanbul, where Ayse and her two sisters grew up. Their father encouraged them to get good educations so that they would not have to be dependent on men.

Ayse entered the University of Istanbul in 1971, majoring in so-ciology. She soon became involved in socialist politics on campus, serving as the editor of the Turkish progressive newspaper *Young Socialist* in 1975. She also helped organize Ilerici Kadinlar Dernegi, the Progressive Women's Organization of Turkey, and was a founding member of the Turkish Peace Association. The Turkish government did not then, and still does not, take kindly to political opposition. As a result of her political work, in 1979 she was tried and sentenced to prison.

To avoid incarceration, she went into hiding, changing her name, using a false identity card, and moving often. By 1983, the police were cracking down, rooting out dissidents, and she knew she would not be able to hide much longer. Using a false passport she escaped to England.

Once in London, she did not stop her activism, helping to found the Turkish Community Center with which she still works. In 1989 she returned to college in London to complete her degree in sociology. She is still active in the struggle for refugee rights in Europe, working with the Turkish Community Center and the Hackney Refugee Training Consortium.

MARY TeRRELL

Black Suffragette

MARY TERRELL was probably the most prominent Black woman advocating suffrage in the late nineteenth and early twentieth century. Terrell's parents were both wealthy. Her father, a former slave, had become one of the wealthiest Black men in the United States as a saloonkeeper, banker, and real estate dealer in Memphis. Her mother was a dressmaker and owned one of the most popular beauty salons in town.

Because of her parents' financial success, Terrell led a privileged life, but she was not free from experiences of prejudice. Once when she accompanied her father on a business trip, the train conductor tried to remove her from a coach reserved for whites. She was even more devastated when she found out her parents and grandparents had been slaves, a fact her family had tried to hide from her.

Educational opportunities in Memphis were limited for a young Black girl, so her parents sent her away to school when she was six. After high school she attended Oberlin College, then started teaching at Wilberforce University in Ohio. After a year she moved to Washington, D.C., to teach high school.

She married in 1891, resigning her position as a teacher, but she was not idle. With her husband's approval she began a full-time career in the Black women's club movement. In 1892 she and seven other educated Black Washington women formed the Colored Women's League, a group dedicated to bettering the Black community. They started an evening school for adults and a day nursery for the children of working mothers, and constantly sought to inform the public about the progress of the Black race.

At this time, Black clubwomen could not join the National Council of Women or the General Federation of Women's Clubs. These groups did not accept "clubs composed of women with a racial origin different from white." So Terrell began to work for the formation of a national body of Black women's clubs. Eventually the National Association of Colored Women (NACW) was formed, and Terrell was elected the first president. She became one of the most visible Black women in the country, and the NACW, under Terrell's leadership, became the leading Black women's organization. In her role as president she was invited to attend meetings of white women's suffrage groups; in 1900 the NACW was accepted as an affiliate member of the mostly white National Council of Women.

As the twentieth century began, Terrell was spending most of her time as a lecturer, writer, suffrage activist, and member of the District of Columbia Board of Education. She gained a national reputation as a lecturer, speaking to the National American Women's Suffrage Association (NAWSA) and the National Congress of Mothers. She attended suffrage meetings, marched on suffrage picket lines, and lectured on suffrage before both white and Black audiences. She was one of only a few Black women to address the NAWSA, which was led by Susan B. Anthony.

Despite her popularity as a speaker before these white groups, she was never elected to office. In fact, she was not even welcome as a member. There was no significant Black presence in the suffrage movement. White women were very aware that they could not fight for Black suffrage and gain support in the South, so they downplayed any connection to Black women. At a major women's suffrage parade in Washington, D.C., in the summer of 1913, the organizers tried to have Black participants march separately at the end of the parade, instead of by home state or profession, as was customary.

Despite the evident prejudice, Terrell remained a strong supporter of suffrage. After the suffrage amendment was passed, she continued to fight for the rights of Black women voters as president of the Colored Women's Republican League.

Terrell also continued her lecturing, because she believed that educating whites, who were so uninformed about Blacks, was the way to achieve interracial understanding. In 1904 she delivered a speech at the International Congress of Women in Berlin, in German, one of three languages she spoke fluently. She also wrote for periodicals, contributing articles and short stories that exposed lynchings, chain gangs, and the disfranchisement of African Americans. In 1913 she was a founding member of the NAACP Washington branch.

In the last two decades of her life, her methods changed. She had become extremely frustrated at the economic hardships African Americans had faced during the Depression and was outraged that Blacks were fighting for democracy abroad during World War II but were denied it at home. She became a militant activist, working to end discrimination in the United States. Realizing that her previous methods of interracial dialogue had not been effective, she took to picketing, boycotting, and sit-ins. In February 1950, at the age of eighty-six, she joined a group attempting to desegregate a restaurant in Washington, D.C. When the group was refused service, they filed suit. During the three-year court battle that ensued, she continued to fight to desegre-

> However much the white women of the country need suffrage, for many reasons which will immediately occur to us, colored women need it more.
>
> **—Mary Terrell**

gate other facilities. In June 1953 the court ruled that segregation in eating facilities in Washington, D.C., was unconstitutional. She died on July 24, 1954, two months after the U.S. Supreme Court passed its historic decision in *Brown v. Board of Education,* which ended segregation in the nation's schools.

MaRY SHADD CARY
The Power of the Press

MARY SHADD CARY was the first Black American female editor, publisher, and investigative reporter. She was introduced to activism by her father, a well-to-do shoemaker and property owner in Wilmington, Delaware, who was also a leader in the Underground Railroad. Because Mary could not attend school in Delaware because of her race, the Shadd family moved to West Chester, Pennsylvania, where they enrolled her in a Quaker school. After completing her schooling, Mary was a teacher for eleven years. Like many other Blacks, Mary and her brother moved to Canada following the passage of the Fugitive Slave Law and the two settled in Windsor. There, she published several pamphlets promoting Black immigration to Canada. Life in Canada was not the Promised Land for Blacks—white prejudice was alive and well there—but it was better than being subject to re-enslavement.

Blacks in Canada fell into two philosophical camps, just as

they did in the United States. There were the separatists who believed that integration would inevitably fail and that Blacks should maintain their own separate communities based on common culture and experience. They had a strong voice in the Black settlements in Canada. And there were the assimilationists who believed that Blacks would attain full equality only when they were integrated into white society.

Mary fell into the integrationist camp, which put her into conflict with the dominant segregationists. She was strongly opposed to some of the techniques of one of the separatist organizations, the Refugee Home Society, that used agents to collect funds, clothing, and land for fugitive slaves. In Mary's view this was begging, completely the opposite of her goal of integrated self-sufficiency.

In order to state her views more publicly and to more effectively reply to her critics, she took a step that was a first for a Black woman in North America: she published a newspaper. In 1853, she published the first edition of the *Provincial Freeman,* and became its editor, establishing the newspaper's headquarters in Toronto. In 1855 she attended the National Negro Convention in Philadelphia, becoming the first Black woman admitted as a correspondent.

She married Thomas Cary in 1856 and had two children, all the while continuing to publish her paper. Plagued with financial difficulties, she shut down the paper in 1859. This calamity was followed swiftly by her husband's death. Mary went back to teaching, first in Canada and then in the United States when she returned there in 1863, during the Civil War. Wanting to do her part for the war effort, she became a recruiter for the Union Army.

At the end of the Civil War she debated about returning to Canada, but many Blacks had become disillusioned with Canada's brand of racism and were returning to the United States. She decided to remain to help educate freed slaves, eventually opening a school in Washington, D.C., while preaching self-help and integration to biracial audiences. Not content with what she had achieved so far, she went to Howard University Law School in the evening, supporting herself by teaching in the day. After receiving her degree, she opened a law office in Washington, D.C. One of her outstanding accomplishments as a lawyer was winning herself the right to vote after she challenged the House of Representatives Judiciary Committee. She was one of the few women who voted in federal elections during the Reconstruction Period.

Mary was also active in the fight for women's rights, organizing the Colored Women's Progressive Franchise Association in 1880. She remained active on the lecture circuit, speaking out for equal rights for Blacks and women, until her death at age seventy.

RUBYE ROBiNSoN
▲▲▲▲▲▲▲▲▲▲▲▲▲▲▲▲▲▲▲▲▲▲▲▲▲▲▲▲▲▲▲▲
Young, Gifted, and Black

RUBYE ROBINSON was an independent female from the start. When her sister began kindergarten in the 1940s, Rubye, then three years old, insisted on joining her. She was in first grade at age four, staying ahead of her age group throughout elementary school, and at the age of sixteen she enrolled at Spelman College in Atlanta.

By then she was already politically active. She had been deeply affected by television coverage of older people walking during the bus boycott in Montgomery, Alabama. She joined other students in a sit-in campaign against segregated restaurants. In April 1960 she attended the founding meeting of the Student Non-Violent Coordinating Committee (SNCC) in Raleigh, North Carolina. Her involvement in the civil rights movement never wavered from that point.

In February 1961 she was arrested at a sit-in in Rock Hill, South Carolina, and was among those who chose not to pay their fines and, instead, remained in jail. This tactic served two purposes: it saved scarce bail money and served to solidify the commitment of the demonstrators. In the spring of 1961 she answered the call for reinforcements from the Freedom Riders jailed in Birmingham, Alabama. The integrated bus rides had been started by the Congress of Racial Equality (CORE) and continued by SNCC to break the hold of Jim Crow on interstate travel in the South. By law and custom, Blacks were relegated to the back seats of public transportation and were not allowed to sit with whites while traveling in the South.

On May 20, 1961, she joined nine other students on a bus ride from Nashville, Tennessee, to Montgomery; the bus was attacked by a white mob. On May 24 she and eleven other Freedom Riders boarded a bus for Jackson, Mississippi, where they were arrested for breach of peace. Again Rubye refused to pay her fine, choosing instead to serve her two-month jail sentence.

When she was released, she went to McComb, Mississippi, to join the voter registration project there. That fall she returned to Spelman College, but continued her participation in SNCC. In the spring of 1963, at the age of twenty-one, she began working for SNCC full-time, in a post she held until 1967, as administrative assistant to executive secretary James Forman. She organized student recruits, provided for the day-to-day needs of field staff, and ran the Sojourner Motor Fleet, cars used in the voter registration drives.

In the fall of 1964 SNCC held a staff retreat to discuss its future direction. During that time, Rubye made policy decisions and saw to the day-to-day running of the organization. She later made a trip to Africa that profoundly affected her and deepened her commitment to Black nationalism. She was among the first to urge SNCC to develop ties with Africa.

Rubye also took part in the fight for equality within SNCC. The leadership of the organization was predominantly male; women were confined primarily to clerical work. Rubye participated in a sit-in in James Forman's office to demand a greater role for the women on staff.

In November 1964 she married Clifford Robinson, the chief mechanic for the Sojourner Motor Fleet. They had a son the following year. Marriage did not slow her down. In the summer of 1966 she took over from James Forman as executive secretary of SNCC, at a time when chairman Stokely Carmichael was moving the organization toward Black nationalism, a direction Rubye strongly supported.

But her fight for civil rights was cut short. She became ill with leukemia in January 1967 and died the following October at the age of twenty-five. Forman remembered her as "one of the few genuine revolutionaries in the Black liberation movement."

FAUZiYA KASSINDjA and WARIS DiRIE

▲▲▲▲▲▲▲▲▲▲▲▲▲▲▲▲▲▲▲▲▲

African Sheroes

FEMALE GENITAL MUTILATION (FGM) is a traditional practice in many parts of Africa. But it is becoming increasingly controversial as information about the practice is revealed throughout the world through the efforts of women such as Fauziya Kassindja and Waris Dirie.

Fauziya Kassindja's father, a Togo businessman, protected his daughters from the custom. He died suddenly when she was sixteen, and her much more traditional uncle became head of the family. She woke up one morning in 1994 to find out that she was to be married that day to a man almost thirty years her senior and who had three other wives—and that she was to be circumcised two days later.

Her mother and sister helped her to escape Togo. Then, using a false passport, she traveled to Germany, where she knew no one. A woman she met at the airport took her in until she was able to arrange to go to the United States, where she hoped to gain political asylum. When she arrived in the United States, she presented her false passport, explaining that she had used it to flee her country to avoid circumcision and asked for asylum. Instead she was held in detention by the Immigration and Naturalization Service for seventeen months, where she was shackled, strip-searched, held in solitary confinement for nineteen days after she was misdiagnosed with tuberculosis, and then put in a cell with a murderer. Her eyesight began to fail and she developed a peptic ulcer.

A student attorney heard her story and took on her case, but an immigration judge denied Kassindja's request for asylum. She was facing deportation back to Togo. Her attorney then sought the support of the Baha'i community and other human rights organizations. The International Human Rights Law Clinic took Kassindja's case on appeal, and nationwide publicity ensued. In 1996 Kassindja became the first woman granted asylum because of the threat of genital mutilation, setting a national precedent. Now asylum can be granted for gender-based

I've got to do it not only for me but for all the little girls in the world who are going through it now. Not hundreds, not thousands, but millions of girls are living with it and dying from it. It's too late to change my own circumstances, the damage has already been done; but maybe I can help save somebody else.

—**Waris Dirie**

persecution, such as rape, forced marriage, FGM, or forced prostitution. Since then many countries, including Togo, have passed laws outlawing female circumcision.

Kassindja remains in the United States. She works for the Tahirih Justice Center in Falls Church, Virginia, which provides assistance to immigrant women. She has told her story in the book *Do They Hear You When You Cry?*

Nearly all of the women in Somalia have been circumcised, believing that no man will have them if they aren't. Waris Dirie begged her mother to let her be like the other girls, so when she was five years old, her mother held her down while a gypsy performed the operation with no anesthetic, using a dirty, dull razor blade. She was sewn up with thorns and thread, left only with a tiny opening for urinating. When she began to menstruate, it was so painful that she often fainted.

When she was thirteen, she ran away from an arranged marriage to a man four times her age. She crossed the desert on foot, arriving at an aunt's in Mogadishu. Soon she moved with an uncle to London, where she was discovered by a photographer who saw her working at McDonald's and was struck by her beauty. The daughter of desert nomads was soon a top model, walking the runways of Paris and Milan and appearing in the 1987 James Bond movie, *The Living Daylights*. While in London, she had corrective surgery to reopen her vagina.

In 1993 she moved to New York and continued her modeling career. There she met Dana Murray, and a few years later had her son, Aleeke. When a writer from *Marie Claire* magazine interviewed her for an article, Waris decided to use the opportunity to speak out about female genital mutilation. The article received a tremendous response, and she was interviewed by Barbara Walters for a segment on *20/20*. Someone at the UN saw the show, which led to her appointment as a special ambassador by the United Nations in 1997. She has put her modeling career on hold to travel the world working to bring an end to the practice of female genital mutilation.

FEMALE GENITAL MUTILATION

Female genital mutilation has been practiced for more than 4,000 years and currently occurs in twenty-eight African countries and to a lesser extent in the Middle East and Asia. The simplest form involves removing the hood of the clitoris so that the woman cannot enjoy sex. In the most severe form, infibulation, the clitoris, labia minor, and most of the labia major are removed and the wound is sewn up, leaving a tiny hole for urination and menstruation. Later, after marriage, the husband will force himself into this tiny opening. According to the World Health Organization, this surgery has been performed on 130 million women and young girls. An additional 2 million are at risk for this surgery each year. The operation is usually performed with no anesthetic by a village woman using razor blades, knives, scissors, broken glass, or sharp stones. Complications can include shock, infection, tetanus, HIV infection, and even death. And the number of women being subjected to this practice is growing. Africans who emigrate take the practice with them. Expatriate African communities will save enough money to bring a circumciser from Africa to their new country, where they will circumcise a group of girls all at once. In the United States, Congress has passed legislation outlawing the practice, but it continues. The custom is difficult to eradicate as many people erroneously believe it is a religious necessity dictated by the Koran.

WANGARi MAATHaI

▲▲▲▲▲▲▲▲▲▲▲▲▲▲▲▲▲▲▲▲▲▲▲▲▲▲▲▲▲▲▲▲▲▲▲

A Green Thumb for the World

WANGARI MAATHAI has become the Johnny Appleseed of Africa. She was born in 1940 in Kenya, in a rural African village near the Great Rift Valley. As a small child, she watched her mother and the other women of the village perform the traditional tasks of growing, harvesting, and preparing food for the village. Early on, her mother taught her a deep respect for the natural world. Wangari made this respect her own and loved to observe nature.

As part of the assistance the United States gave to Kenya in 1960 while that country prepared for its transition to freedom from British rule, several hundred Kenyan students were offered scholarships to U.S. colleges. Wangari was awarded one and attended Mount St. Scholastica College in Atchison, Kansas, majoring in biology. She went on to earn a master of science degree from the University of Pittsburgh in 1965. When Wangari completed college, she returned to Africa and became the first Kenyan woman to receive a doctorate from the University of Nairobi. She followed this achievement by becoming the first Kenyan woman appointed to be a professor and to become a department chairperson, as head of the anatomy department.

After marrying a member of the Kenyan Parliament and having three children, she worked hard in her husband's district to improve conditions for his poor constituents and championed women's rights. Her activism and academic success contributed to the demise of her marriage. "Perhaps I grew up and started getting into the limelight at a time when academic success for a woman was not common," she reflected. "This put a lot of pressure on a

Wangari Maathi

man who was influenced by other men against a successful woman. But that was in the 1970s. . . . I don't think that would have happened now."

After her divorce, she resigned her job at the university in order to run for Parliament. Later she was forced to abandon her campaign, and the university refused to return her to her position. No other university would take her, and she was forced to live off her savings. While volunteering at the National Council of Women in Kenya, she turned her attention to the environment and decided to focus her attention on planting trees. Although others thought she was crazy to waste her education on such a venture, she was certain that she could make a difference with her efforts.

On June 5, 1977, World Environment Day, Wangari and her supporters planted seven trees in a public park, marking the beginning of the Green Belt Movement. But why trees? To begin with, 97 percent of the trees in Kenya had been destroyed. With that loss came problems of air pollution, which trees help clean; a loss of food supplied by trees, such as fruit and nuts; soil erosion; and desertification. These changes in the environment were changing how people lived. Since cooking traditional foods took a long time and used up a lot of firewood, which was becoming scarce, the women started buying and using more processed and refined foods. This diet was less healthy, especially for children. Wangari saw the planting of trees as a solution to all these problems.

In Kenya, 80 percent of the farmers are women. Besides growing food, they take care of the animals and gather firewood. Wangari began her campaign by bringing in foresters to teach women how to plant trees. They learned how to gather seeds and start seedlings, which they then gave to other farmers and schoolchildren to plant. The women farmers would have a source of firewood and their soil would be protected from erosion. The schoolchildren used their seedlings to plant wind breaks around their schools.

The Green Belt Movement has expanded throughout Africa. Since its inception, more than 80,000 women have planted more than 15 million trees. An attendant for the nursery is chosen by the women of the area but paid by Green Belt, which also pays "rangers," usually the elderly or the handicapped, to care for the seedlings after they are planted. A woman receives a small financial reward for each tree that survives. Although it is a very small amount, it is nevertheless helpful to each woman.

> We should understand nature's laws if we expect her to shower us with earthly blessings. We must stop the over-exploitation and the plundering. We must begin to care.
> —**Wangari Maathai**

For her work, Wangari has received the Right Livelihood Award, the United Nations Environmental Program Global 500 Award, a "Woman of the World" citation from Diana, Princess of Wales, an honorary degree from Williams College in Massachusetts, and the Goldman Environment Prize. But some of her political stances in recent years have made her unpopular with the government in her country. She has been targeted by the ruling party, and the Green Belt Movement has been thrown out of its government offices. Wangari now works from home.

In 1992, during a protest march for the release of political prisoners, Wangari was clubbed unconscious by the police and was hospitalized. This did nothing to curb her activism. Besides continuing her work with the Green Belt Movement, she has become an outspoken advocate of human rights in her native country. In 1998 she ran a losing campaign for the presidency of Kenya. She was physically attacked again in January 1999 while she and a group of twenty others were attempting to plant trees in the Karura Forest near Nairobi as part of a protest against real estate development in the area.

Despite all of the opposition she has encountered, Wangari continues to be a staunch advocate for the environment and human rights and is hopeful for the future.

CHARLOTTE FORTEN GRiMkE

Pioneering Educator

Charlotte Forten Grimke was born a free Black to the wealthy, activist Forten family of Philadelphia in 1837. Indoctrinated into the abolitionist movement at her parents' knees, she early on became determined to contribute to the liberation of all Black people. As a child she had been tutored at home because she was denied admission to Philadelphia schools due to her race. When she was sixteen, she moved in with a Salem, Massachusetts, family in order to attend the integrated schools there. She was the only nonwhite out of 200 students at her school.

The family in Salem, like her own, was adamantly abolitionist. During her stay there she met many of the luminaries of the abolitionist movement, such as William Lloyd Garrison and Wendell Phillips. But even in Massachusetts her life was not free from discrimination. However, the prejudice she witnessed against herself and others only strengthened her resolve. She was an active member of the Salem Female Anti-Slavery Society. During her stay in Salem she began writing poetry, much of it on antislavery themes. Her works were published in antislavery periodicals such as the *Liberator* and the *National Anti-Slavery Standard*.

I wonder that every colored person is not a misanthrope. Surely we have everything to make us hate mankind.

—Charlotte Grimke

While continuing her support of the abolitionist movement, Charlotte began teaching in 1856. Two years later she was forced to return to Philadelphia because of a recurring bout of tuberculosis. When the Civil War began in 1861, she saw an opportunity to work for a hastened end to slavery. Thousands of destitute and illiterate slaves were being freed by the Union troops, and the government began recruiting young men and women to teach and prepare them for citizenship. Charlotte eagerly donated her services to educating her people, becoming the first Black teacher to be hired and sent to the Sea Islands off the coast of South Carolina. The Union Army troops had routed the planters from the islands, leaving behind 10,000 slaves. Other slaves gravitated to the islands when they heard of the emancipation occurring there.

Here she was immersed in a different world from that of her upbringing. Conditions were primitive and harsh. The Black people she taught were very different from her; they even spoke a different language, a patois of English and African words. Charlotte and two other teachers taught the children in the afternoons and the adults in the evenings when they returned from their work in the fields. During her two-year stay, Charlotte wrote several articles for the *Atlantic Monthly*, chronicling her teaching experience. Of her charges she wrote, "I never before saw children so eager. . . . Coming to school is a constant delight and recreation to them. They come here as other children go to play. . . . Many of the grown people are desirous of learning to read. It is wonderful how a people who have been so long crushed to the earth . . . can have so great a desire for knowledge, and such a capability for attaining it." When Charlotte left the Sea Islands for Philadelphia in 1864, 2,000 children were enrolled in school and thousands of adults were becoming literate.

Upon her return to Philadelphia, she continued to teach and also gained a reputation as a writer and poet. In 1878, at the age of forty-one, she married Reverend Francis J. Grimke, who was also fighting for racial equality. Many of the leaders of the abolition movement attended their wedding. Charlotte apparently enjoyed the duties of a minister's wife, teaching Sunday school classes and founding a women's missionary group. Until her death on July 23,

1913, she continued to champion the cause of equal rights for Black people.

MABEL STAUPeRS
▲▲▲▲▲▲▲▲▲▲▲▲▲▲▲▲▲▲▲▲▲▲▲▲▲▲▲▲▲

Leading the Way in Nursing

MABEL STAUPERS was born in Barbados, West Indies, in 1890 and in 1903 migrated to the United States with her parents, settling in Harlem in New York City. After completing high school in 1914, she enrolled in the Freedmen's Hospital School of Nursing (now the Howard University College of Nursing) in Washington, D.C., graduating with honors three years later. Since the majority of hospital nurses' training schools would not admit Black women, the African American community, as in so many other areas of life, created a parallel system of hospitals and nursing training schools, along with separate professional societies and organizations.

She began her career as a private-duty nurse, but that part of her career was brief. In 1920, with two Black physicians, she founded the Booker T. Washington Sanitarium, the first inpatient treatment center in Harlem for Black patients with tuberculosis. It was one of a handful of facilities in the city that allowed Black physicians to treat patients.

For twelve years Staupers was the executive secretary for the Harlem Committee of the New York Tuberculosis and Health Association. She worked tirelessly to make sure that money and resources were available for minority groups afflicted with tuberculosis.

In 1934 she became executive secretary of the National Association of Colored Graduate Nurses (NACGN). She and the organization's president, Estelle Osborne, fought for the integration of Black nurses. The start of World War II aided their struggle. The demand for more nurses helped them thrust the plight of Black nurses into the national spotlight. Tired by the arduous fight for integration, she resigned her position with the NACGN in 1946, but shortly she was back on the front lines, working for the integration of Black women into the American Nurses' Association (ANA). That was accomplished in 1948, and the members of the NACGN voted it out of existence in 1949, its functions assumed by the ANA. In 1951 the NAACP awarded Staupers the NAACP's Spingarn Medal for outstanding achievement by a Black person.

ANNiE ONeTA PLUMMER

The Dictionary Lady

A HOUSEWIFE FROM Savannah, Georgia, Annie Plummer made a difference in the lives of thousands of schoolchildren. Raised in Savannah, she quit school in the ninth grade after she became pregnant. To support herself and her daughter, she became a housekeeper. Eventually she was able to return to school, earning her high school diploma in 1978.

Annie was active in her community and passionate about Black history. Her life took the road less traveled one morning in 1992 when she noticed that the elementary schoolchildren walking by her house didn't have books. It occurred to her that if they had a basic book like a dictionary to stimulate their interest in learning, it could change their lives.

Taking $50 of her own money, she bought thirty pocket dictionaries and started passing them out on her street corner. She inscribed in each one, "A mind is a terrible thing to waste. I challenge you not to waste yours." A local newspaper printed an article about her efforts, and people started sending her donations. She also sold "Dictionary Lady" T-shirts and organized a Dictionary Walkathon to raise funds. Churches and community organizations helped buy and distribute more dictionaries. Her goal in 1995 was to make sure every third-grade student in Chatham County, about 4,000 children, had a free dictionary. By 1996 she had surpassed that goal by 13,000.

Her fame spread. She was featured in *Southern Living* and *People* magazines and praised by General Norman H. Schwarzkopf and others. There are now six more Dictionary Ladies across the country. The Dictionary Lady Foundation was incorporated in Savannah in 1997 to assist the branch organizations.

Ms. Plummer died in December 1999. At that time, 32,800 dictionaries had been put into the hands of schoolchildren because of her efforts. Her daughter is continuing the work her mother started.

POWERFUL
POLITICOS
AND BOLD
BUSINESS
WOMEN

 ERTHA
PASCAL-TROUiLLOT

Presiding Over a Troubled Land

S INCE ITS INCEPTION in 1804 through a slave rebellion, Haiti is a
country that has been torn by violent power struggles. Military
coups and dictatorships have been the norm. In 1957, Francois
"Papa Doc" Duvalier was elected president, declaring himself
president-for-life in 1964.

Ertha Pascal was a teenager at the time, the ninth of ten children. Her father died when she was young, leaving the family dependent on her mother's meager earnings as a seamstress and
whatever her older siblings could earn. Although they were poor,
their mother raised them with respect for family, religion, and
work.

Ertha was an excellent student. Ernst Trouillot, a lawyer and
history teacher twenty-one years her senior, took an interest in

her education, teaching her history and tutoring her in French, the language of the ruling class. He evidently took an interest in her personally as well. Shortly after she earned her law degree in 1971, they were married.

In 1986, the Duvalier regime was overturned. During the next two years four different men ruled Haiti. In 1988, by now a widow, Ertha became the first woman to sit on Haiti's Supreme Court. In 1990, after a series of coups led twelve of Haiti's political parties to form a coalition to create a provisional government, she became interim president of Haiti. The leaders of the coalition requested that Pascal-Trouillot accept the position, and reluctantly she did so.

She was not a dictator, sharing power with a committee that could overturn her decisions. After her inauguration, violence in the streets decreased and foreign aid resumed. More important, in a country given to military coups, the army seemed to support her.

However, her presidency was tainted by charges that she had risen to power through her support of the Duvaliers and that she was stealing from the national treasury. She was also hampered by the fact that she had not been elected and had little grassroots support. True to her promise, elections were held less than a year after she was installed, and Jean-Bertrand Aristide was elected by a landslide. Some military factions opposed his election; Roger Lafontant, formerly a Duvalier security officer, broke into the presidential mansion and seized Pascal-Trouillot, forcing her to read a statement on Haitian television naming him the new president.

Riots erupted and Lafontant was forced to flee. Aristide was inaugurated as planned. He then had Pascal-Truillot arrested, claiming she had participated in the coup willingly, but she vehemently denied these charges, saying Lafontant had threatened her daughter's life. The charges became moot when Aristide was overthrown eight months after his inauguration.

Various factions continue to vie for power in Haiti. As for Pascal-Trouillot, she saw her presidency as an interim government and has no ambitions to return to power.

RUtH PERRY
▲▲▲▲▲▲▲▲▲▲▲▲▲▲▲▲▲▲▲▲▲▲▲

Pioneering Head of State

DESPITE THE FACT that, in antiquity, African women had often led their people, African politics has been the domain of men since independence began in the 1960s. Ruth Perry has the distinction of being the first female head of state in modern-day Africa.

She achieved this in 1996 in Liberia, which was being torn apart by civil war. Liberia is a country that was settled by former African American slaves in the early nineteenth century; these ex-slaves held political and economic power over the native population. Conflict between the settlers and the indigenous peoples continues to this day.

Perry's family is part of one of Liberia's indigenous groups, the Vai Muslims. After Perry completed high school, she became an elementary school teacher, married, and had seven children.

In 1971, after all her children had entered school, she went to work for the Chase Manhattan Bank in Monrovia. Political unrest forced Chase Manhattan to close its Liberian offices in 1985, and she lost her job.

By 1980, the indigenous people had reasserted power in the country. A young military officer named Samuel K. Doe was appointed ruler, although civil unrest continued to mount until elections were held in 1985. Doe became president in an election that was probably rigged. In that same election, Ruth Perry was elected to a seat in the Liberian Senate. She remained in this seat until 1989, when she left the senate and opened a retail business, continuing her political activism by participating in several activist organizations, such as Women in Action for Goodwill. She was an outspoken advocate of disarmament.

In the '90s, the conflict between the two opposing groups continued to grow. Thousands were killed and dozens of peace accords were broken by both sides. The fighting reached a head in April 1996, when nearly 3,000 people died in a few weeks. The years of conflict had cost a total of 150,000 lives, and 2.6 million Liberians were homeless. All of the businesses in the capital city of Monrovia had been destroyed.

In August 1996, peacekeeping troops engineered a cease-fire, appointing Perry as the head of the interim government with the approval of the warring factions and most civilian Liberians. Although hesitant, she accepted the position in September 1996. She headed the government until elections were held in July 1997, when Charles Taylor was elected president in another disputed election. She continues to be an ardent advocate for national reconciliation and the rebuilding of her country.

GERTRUDE MONGELLA: MAMA BEIJING

Gertrude Mongella began life in a tiny rural Tanzanian village on an island in Lake Victoria, and has risen to become an influential figure in the women's movement throughout Africa. When she was twelve, she left her home to attend a school run by Maryknoll nuns, who prepared their students to participate in the development of their country when it gained independence. Gertrude entered public life in 1975 when she became a member of the East African Legislative Assembly, and since then, she has held several ministerial posts, including Minister of State for Women's Affairs; Minister of Lands, Natural Resources, and Tourism; Minister Without Portfolio in the President's Office; and Ambassador to India. She has represented Tanzania at numerous international meetings, and in 1989, was Tanzania's representative on the Commission on the Status of Women.

She has been Special Advisor to the UNESCO Director General and is founder of a group called Advocacy for Women in Africa. She was given the nickname Mama Beijing after she was invited by UN Secretary General Boutros Boutros Ghali to chair the Fourth United Nations World Conference on Women in Beijing in September 1995. She continues to lead an active life, dedicating most of her time to issues relating to women, economic development, and the environment.

People who value democracy, people who believe in equality are now saying we must change the world so that women and men working together in equal partnership can really bring about sustainable development during the twenty-first century.

—Gertrude Mongella

SHiRLEY CHISHoLM

Unbought and Unbossed

SHIRLEY CHISHOLM did not set out to create a career in politics, yet she became the first Black woman to be elected to Congress and the first Black woman to run for president of the United States.

A native of Brooklyn, New York, she lived in Barbados with her grandmother until she was almost ten. She was an excellent student, earning scholarships to both Vassar and Oberlin colleges. She chose instead to attend Brooklyn College, graduating in 1946 with a degree in sociology and a minor in Spanish. She worked at Mount Calvary Childcare Center, and attended Columbia University at night, eventually earning an M.A. in child education. It was also at Columbia that she met her husband, Conrad Chisholm.

Had she not joined the Bureau of Child Welfare as a day care specialist in 1959, she might have remained a teacher. Her work with minority women and children increased her concern for the issues affecting them. As her concern increased, so did her activity in Democratic politics. She joined the campaign to elect a Black lawyer to a district court judgeship in New York. In 1960, she helped form the Unity Democratic Club, which supported candidates for the New York State 17th Assembly District. In 1964, she decided to run for the 17th District state representative seat herself and won by a landslide. She served in the state assembly for five years, where she worked tirelessly for legislation to benefit

"In the end, antiBlack, antifemale, and all forms of discrimination are equivalent to the same thing—antihumanism."

"There is little place in the political scheme of things for an independent, creative personality, for a fighter. Anyone who takes that role must pay a price."

"Service is the rent that you pay for room on this Earth."

"Tremendous amounts of talent are being lost to our society just because that talent wears a skirt."

"I was well on the way to forming my present attitude toward politics as it is practiced in the United States; it is a beautiful fraud that has been imposed on the people for years, whose practitioners exchange gilded promises for the most valuable thing their victims own—their votes. And who benefits most? The lawyers."

"Racism is so universal in this country, so widespread and deep-seated, that it is invisible because it is so normal."

"At present, our country needs women's idealism and determination, perhaps more in politics than anywhere else."

"Of my two 'handicaps,' being female put many more obstacles in my path than being Black."

"When morality comes up against profit, it is seldom profit that loses."

"I'm the only one among you who has the balls to run for president." (To the Black Caucus members at the Democratic convention)

"My goal was to shake things up a little. I think I made a dent or two."

"The mere fact that a Black woman dared to run for President . . . is what it was all about. 'It can be done'; that was what I was trying to say, by doing it."

disadvantaged students, establish childcare programs, and aid unemployed domestic workers. Throughout her legislative career, she always considered herself more an advocate than a legislator.

In 1969, she campaigned for the post of congressperson from New York's newly formed 12th Congressional District and won, becoming the first African American congresswoman in U.S. history. During her stay in Congress, she served on the Veterans' Affairs Committee, the Education and Labor Committee, and the influential House Rules Committee. She was a vocal advocate for equal rights for women and minorities and an outspoken critic of U.S. involvement in Vietnam. She was on the Democratic National Committee in 1972 and 1976. In 1970, she published her first book, *Unbought and Unbossed.* Her second, *The Good Fight,* followed in 1973.

In 1972, she became the first Black woman to campaign for the Democratic nomination for president, using the slogan "Unbought and unbossed." She gathered support from those not usually courted by organized politics—women, the elderly, minorities, and gay activists. She ran hard, even though it was certain she could not win, knowing that her campaign served to bring the issues she was concerned with to the attention of the public.

She remained in Congress through the '70s, but she longed to return to her first love, teaching. She retired from Congress

Shirley Chisholm

in February 1982 and accepted a teaching position at Mount Holyoke College, teaching politics and women's studies. Continuing her political activism, she founded the National Political Congress of Black Women in 1984, and in 1993, President Clinton appointed her Ambassador to Jamaica. She continues to be an outspoken advocate of the rights of those on the fringes of power.

MARiA LIBERIA-PETERS

Prime Minister in Paradise

SINCE 1975, Maria Liberia-Peters has been a popular politician in her native country of the Netherlands Antilles, an autonomous region that is part of the Kingdom of the Netherlands. That, however, was not her original calling in life. Born in 1941 in Willenstad, Curaçao, she received a teaching degree in early childhood education and was a kindergarten teacher and an instructor in training college before entering politics.

As a teacher, she became aware of the needs of her students and their families. In order to help, she organized parent groups and joined the

> I've realized that you cannot reach your goal without power. So it's not a nasty word, it's an important word. But you must know what you want to do with that power. Serve mankind, serve for humanity, and then, yes, give me all the power in the world.
>
> **—Maria Liberia-Peters**

National People's Party. In 1975 she was encouraged to run for office and won a seat on the Curaçao island council. For five years she was part of an executive council that met with representatives of Queen Beatrix.

In 1982, she was elected to the legislature of the Netherlands Antilles and also became the Minister of Economic Affairs. The coalition government collapsed in June 1984. In September of that year she agreed to form a new coalition government and became prime minister, a position she held from 1984 until 1986 and then again from 1988 until 1994. Her party lost the elections in 1994, but Liberia-Peters is still a member of Parliament and is the opposition leader.

As a politician she is known for her ability to build consensus. Her opinions and ideas are valued by leaders the world over, and she often participates in gatherings of world politicians.

BENEDiTA da SILVA

▲▲▲▲▲▲▲▲▲▲▲▲▲▲▲▲▲▲▲▲▲▲▲▲▲▲▲▲▲▲▲▲▲▲▲

From Shantytown to Senate

BENEDITA DA SILVA has traveled from the slums of Rio de Janeiro to the halls of Brazil's senate. Her parents had been day laborers in the Minas Gerais area of Brazil, working in exchange for food. Often they did not have enough to feed their twelve children. In 1936, her mother moved with the children to the slums of Rio de

Janeiro, taking in wash to make a living. Her husband joined her after she had managed to get a shack big enough for the whole family. Benedita was born there in 1943. By the time she was seven, Benedita was working, shining shoes, and selling candy after school. She was the only one in her family who learned how to read and write.

When Benedita was fifteen, her mother died. This was a terrible emotional loss for the family, but also a financial one because her mother's earnings had made a big contribution to the family pot. Benedita had to work more and dropped out of school. She also began volunteering with the community literacy and health projects, hoping to get help for her family from these groups. The next year she met Nilton Aldano da Silva, a handyman and house painter. They were married in December 1958. She continued to work with neighborhood groups, organizing literacy classes and working to improve health conditions in the shantytown.

By the time she was twenty, she had two children (two others had died shortly after birth) but was so busy working to feed them that she hardly spent any time with them. Despite all the efforts she and her husband made, sometimes they were all so hungry that she would ties strips of cloth around their stomachs to help ease the hunger pangs.

She worked first as a street vendor, then in a leather belt factory, and later as a janitor at a school. In 1975, she got a job as a clerk at the Department of Transportation. Four years later she took a nurse's aide course and took an additional part-time job at a hospital. It had always bothered her that she hadn't finished high

93

> For me, ideology is not the key issue. Whether you believe in capitalism or socialism as the best social system is really irrelevant. The most important thing is what you do in your everyday life to make the world better.
>
> **—Benedita da Silva**

school, so she began to study at home for the high school equivalency exam, passing it in 1980. She then enrolled in the university to study social work, attending with her twenty-year-old daughter. In 1978, she was voted president of the neighborhood association.

Her husband was a supportive man who loved her very much. But he had a problem with alcohol and died of a stroke when he was only forty-five years old. They had been together for twenty-two years. After his death she became even more involved with the neighborhood association. In 1982, a new political party was being formed. Her friends in the neighborhood association urged her to run for the city council. She went door to door campaigning and spoke to people while she stood on a box in public squares. To everyone's amazement, she won, becoming the first Workers' Party representative in Rio. As the only representative of her party on the council, she was subjected to paternalism and racism from the other members. Following her political beliefs, she employed people from all walks of life and all ethnicities in her office.

In 1986 she was elected a federal deputy to the National Assembly, a post to which she was re-elected four years later. Agnaldo Bezerra dos Santos, better known as Bola, the president of the association, had become her chief political advisor after her successful city council run; six months later, he became her husband. After only five years of marriage, he died of a sudden illness. She was devastated. Many people thought that he was the real power and that this would mark the end of her political career, but she decided to keep going. In 1992, she campaigned for mayor of Rio, but lost by 3 percent of the vote. In 1994, she waged a successful campaign for the Brazilian senate, becoming the first Black woman elected to it.

In 1991, she met actor and activist Pitanga, also a member of Rio's city council, and then married him in a lavish ceremony at the plush Jockey Club. The press had a field day criticizing a representative of a shantytown for having such a lavish affair at such an elite venue and inviting her friends from the favela. Her response was that these spaces had to be open to everyone and that her friends in the shantytown shouldn't only be able to enter a nice restaurant or club when it was time to clean up.

Now the vice governor of the state of Rio de Janeiro, da Silva still lives in the shantytown she was born in and continues to be an outspoken voice for democracy and for the rights of the poor, minorities, and women.

MARY ChARLES
▲▲▲▲▲▲▲▲▲▲▲▲▲▲▲▲▲▲▲▲▲▲▲▲▲▲▲

Iron Lady of the Caribbean

THE FIRST FEMALE prime minister in the English-speaking Caribbean, Mary Charles was born on the island of Dominica in

1919. Her father founded the Penney Bank, making her family one of the wealthiest on the island. After completing her secondary education, she received a B.A. from the University of Toronto and then studied law at the London School of Economics. She returned to Dominica in 1949, and became the first woman lawyer on the island.

In 1968, the government attempted to pass a sedition law that would have dampened dissent against its policies. Charles' political career began with fighting that law and cofounding the Dominica Freedom Party. In 1970, she was appointed to the legislature and then to the House of Assembly in 1975, where she became the leader of the opposition. In 1978, partly through the efforts of her party, Dominica won its freedom from Great Britain.

She became prime minister when her party won the elections of 1980. During her three consecutive terms, from 1980 to 1995, she instituted economic reform and fought government corruption. She also encouraged tourism, although she was determined to preserve the island's ecology. Dominica has no night clubs or casinos and no intention of building any.

In 1995, her party lost the election, and Mary Charles retired from active politics. She is a member of a coalition of former women world leaders who meet periodically at Harvard University to discuss policy issues.

> Even before we had the vote in Dominica I remember the women, my mother being one of them, who'd get together. And they'd tell their husbands straight, "You can't bring that up, man. We don't want that. It's not good for us." They had no vote, but they certainly had the vote in the house.
>
> **—Mary Charles**

96

OMU OKWEI

▲▲▲▲▲▲▲▲▲▲▲▲▲▲▲▲▲▲▲▲

Market Queen

THE YORUBA and Igbo women of Africa have been traders back to antiquity. Women have traditionally dominated the marketing side of the economy, selling surplus produce and home crafts. At market, women shared the latest news and gossip and engaged in the pleasure of bartering and haggling over prices. Traditionally, a female official in each town managed the female aspects of the community, especially the marketplace. Some of these women amassed great wealth and became very influential in politics.

The British failed to honor this system and attempted to convert it to a male-dominated one, causing many conflicts. One of the best known was the Women's War of 1929, an uprising against British taxation led by Igbo female traders, among them Omu Okwei.

Omu Okwei, from Ossonaria in Nigeria, was one of the most powerful Igbo women. She controlled the vast wholesale marketing and distribution system of the Onitsha market between 1900 and 1929. She began by trading palm produce and foodstuffs, then added imported textiles, tobacco, hardware, and other items. She served as an agent for the chiefs and other important men, acquired a fleet of trucks and canoes, loaned money, and traded in currency. She was elected Market Queen, Chairwoman of the Council of Mothers. Unfortunately, she was the last market queen, because after the Women's War the British transferred supervision of trading from the Council of Mothers to male city officials.

COiNCOIN

▲▲▲▲▲▲▲▲▲▲▲▲▲▲▲▲▲▲▲▲▲▲▲▲▲▲▲▲

Savvy Businesswoman

BORN A SLAVE in Natchitoches, Louisiana, in 1742, her birth name was Marie Therese, but she preferred a nickname she was given by her parents—Coincoin, which means "second daughter" in the language of the Ewe people of Africa. When she was in her mid-twenties, her master rented her out to Claude Metoyer as a housekeeper. Already a mother of five at that time, she had ten more children by Claude.

After twenty years of connubial bliss, Claude was pressured by the local clergy to end his relationship with Coincoin and sell her. Instead he purchased her and freed her along with their seventh child. Two years later he freed two more of their children. Their relationship continued for another eight years, during which they had three more children, all born free. In 1786, Claude married a white woman, leaving Coincoin with an annuity and a small plot of land. At the age of forty-four, Coincoin was on her own.

She began by raising tobacco, indigo, cattle, and turkeys on her small property. Then in 1794, she purchased a land grant from Spain, adding 640 acres to her property, and started a cattle ranch. She prospered and used her money to begin liberating the rest of her children and grandchildren. Over the next twenty years, she tracked them down in Louisiana and Texas. She was unable to free one daughter, but her grandchildren by that daughter were freed.

Claude Metoyer still held four of their children in slavery. At age sixty, Coincoin traded her annuity from him for their freedom. She and her family continued to prosper. When she died, she left 2,000 acres and 50 slaves. Her children and grandchildren, through diligent hard work, increased that to 20,000 acres with a dozen manor houses, a school, a church, and 500 slaves. Indeed, the Metoyers were the largest Black family in the United States to own slaves.

The end of the Civil War and the emancipation of the slaves affected the Metoyer holdings like any other plantation in the South. The family's fortunes declined. Melrose Plantation, the only estate from their large holdings that is still intact, was made a National Historic Landmark in 1975.

EUfROSINA HiNARD

Freeing Slaves Her Way

EUfROSINA HINARD was an unusual businesswoman, to say the least. She made her living buying and renting out slaves, but was more than willing to let them buy their freedom. Little is known about her early life other than that she was born in New Orleans in 1777 to a white man and a freed Black woman. At the age of

fourteen she was *placéed* (committed) to the Spaniard Don Nico-
las Vidal, the military legal counselor to the territory's governor.
This was not an unusual arrangement in the Spanish colonies.
Just as in the French colonies, interracial marriage was outlawed.
A form of de facto marriage called *plaçage* or *concubinato* was
practiced instead. This gave the woman and their children some
political, legal, economic, and social protection.

Eufrosina had two daughters with Vidal. He moved the family
to Spanish Pensacola in what is now Florida after Louisiana was
ceded to the United States in 1803 through the Louisiana Purchase.
He died there in 1806, leaving his estate and its slaves to Eufrosina
and their daughters. She rented out the slaves or let them live out,
a portion of their income coming to her.

Under the Spanish government, slaves had the right to purchase their freedom. After the Spanish territories were ceded to
the United States, slaves no longer had this right, and freedom became more and more difficult to achieve. Eufrosina had been a
Spanish subject most of her life, and held the Spanish view that
slavery was an unfortunate condition and that all slaves had the
right to buy their freedom. The states may have prevented manu-
mission, but Eufrosina continued the practice. She regularly
bought slaves and then allowed them to buy their freedom by
paying her their purchase price, plus interest. Her actions challenged the deeply held Southern notion that slaves had no rights
and that slavery was a natural condition.

MAGGiE LENA WALkER
▲▲▲▲▲▲▲▲▲▲▲▲▲▲▲▲▲▲▲▲▲▲▲▲▲▲▲▲
First Woman Banker

MAGGIE LENA WALKER was an activist in many arenas, but she is most well known for being the first woman banker in the United States.

Her mother worked for the famous Union spy, Elizabeth Van Lew, and her father was an Irish-born newspaperman. Her parents were never married, and eventually her mother married the butler in the Van Lew home. When Maggie was nine, her stepfather was discovered drowned in the river after being missing for five days. It was called a suicide, but Maggie's family assumed he was murdered.

Her mother worked as a laundress to support her two children, while making sure that they received an education. Maggie's all-Black school had an outstanding faculty who were also community leaders. Their example rubbed off on the budding businesswoman. After graduation she became a schoolteacher, giving up that career when she married in 1886. Maggie and her husband had three sons over the next seven years and adopted a daughter.

Maggie Lena Walker had joined Good Idea Council No. 16 of the Independent Order of St. Luke while she was in school. Such organizations were very important in Black life, providing care for the sick and burial insurance. These organizations began evolving into Black insurance companies in the 1890s. Walker had been a delegate to several St. Luke conventions and held various positions in the local organization. Her business career began at the 1895 convention when she proposed the formation of a Juvenile Division, headed by a Council of Matrons. Her resolution was passed, and she was elected Grand Matron, a position she held for the rest of her life. The Juvenile Division touched the lives of tens of thousands of children, teaching racial pride, thrift, and responsibility.

During this time it was difficult for Blacks to obtain bank loans for homes or for businesses. Walker recognized the need for a Black bank, so that Black people could be self-sufficient. When twenty-five councils in Richmond, Virginia, formed a joint stock company in order to purchase property to build a headquarters building, Walker was named secretary of the board. The building was erected in 1903 and housed the central organization, the Right Worthy Grand Council, with Walker serving as secretary. She headed a massive membership drive, preaching economic independence for the Black community, encouraging women to enter the business world, and urging Black people to support Black businesses. Eventually the council started publishing a newspaper and established a bank and a store.

Walker prepared herself for the next step in her career by spending some time each day for several months at the Merchants' National Bank of Richmond. At the age of twenty-seven, she became the first woman bank president in the United States when the St. Luke Penny Savings Bank opened in 1903. It was about this time that she bought the large house that became home for her extended family, including her sons and their brides. It is now a national historic site.

Changes in banking regulations forced the bank to separate from the Order. Other Black banks failed, and by the beginning of the Great Depression, St. Luke Bank and Trust was the only Black bank in Richmond. It has continued to prosper to the present day.

Banking was not Walker's only endeavor. She joined the National Association of Colored Women in 1912 and was at different times chair of the business, finance, and budget committees. She was also a member of the executive committee until she died. Walker was on the board of trustees of the Frederick Douglass Home, helped found and run the Industrial School for Colored Girls, founded and served as lifelong president of Richmond's Council of Colored Women, was one of the founders of Virginia's Negro Organization Society, was on the board of the forerunner to the Richmond branch of the Urban League, and was a board member of the national NAACP from 1923 until she died.

> I was not born with a silver spoon in my mouth, but instead, with a clothes basket upon my head.
>
> **—Maggie Lena Walker**

She began to lose the use of her legs in the late 1920s and spent the last years of her life in a wheelchair, but that scarcely slowed her down. Nicknamed the "Lame Lioness," she died in 1934 after a remarkable life of community involvement.

Successful Scientists

ROGER ARLiNER YoUNG

▲▲▲▲▲▲▲▲▲▲▲▲▲▲▲▲▲▲▲▲▲▲▲▲▲▲▲▲▲▲▲▲

Trying to Make It

S OMETIMES THE PRESSURES on Black women are just too much, even given talent and assistance. Such is the story of Roger Arliner Young, the first Black woman to obtain a Ph.D. in zoology. She was born in Clifton Forge, Virginia, and grew up in Burgettstown, Pennsylvania. In 1916 she entered Howard University and, while taking her first classes with him in 1921, met Ernest Just, head of the zoology department and a prominent Black biologist. She did not do well, but Just saw some talent in her and became her mentor.

She received her bachelor's degree in 1923, after which she was hired under Just's tutelage as an assistant professor of zoology at Howard. He also helped her find funding to attend graduate school. In 1924 she began studies at the University of Chicago part-time, and her grades improved greatly. She started publishing her research: her first article appeared in September 1924. She completed her studies for a master's degree in zoology in 1926.

In 1927, at Just's invitation, she worked with him at the Marine Biological Laboratory in Woods Hole, Massachusetts, during the summer. Starting in 1929, she would stand in for Just as head of the Howard zoology department when he traveled to Europe on grant projects. In the fall of 1929, she began work on her Ph.D., but she failed her qualifying exams in 1930.

Roger Arliner Young

Although she had been successful at both research and teaching, she had a heavy teaching load and few financial resources. She had very little money and had to care for her mother. She broke under the strain and disappeared, keeping her whereabouts secret. Eventually she returned to Howard and to Woods Hole, but the temperature of her relationship with Just dropped considerably. He began to ease her out of her position in 1933, amid rumors of a romance between them and accusations from both sides. Things came to a head in 1936 and she was fired, supposedly because she was missing classes and had mistreated lab equipment.

She took this downturn and made it into an opportunity. She went to the University of Pennsylvania to begin work on her doctorate, which she earned in 1940, becoming the first African American woman to receive a doctorate in zoology. She taught at several Black colleges in the South from 1940 until the early 1960s, when again her mental health broke. She was hospitalized at the Mississippi State Mental Asylum. In 1962 she was discharged and went to Southern University in New Orleans. She died there, alone and impoverished, on November 9, 1964.

Evelyn Granville's career in mathematics and computer programming is filled with accomplishments. She graduated from Smith College in 1945 summa cum laude and Phi Beta Kappa, then earned a Ph.D. in mathematics from Yale University in 1949. In 1956 she was hired by IBM and worked on projects for NASA, making her a pioneer in both computer technology and space flight. She worked on orbit computations and computer procedures for the *Vanguard* and *Mercury* projects, then went on to provide technical support to other NASA missions in trajectory analysis, orbit computation, and digital computer techniques. In 1967 she took a teaching position at the University of Southern California in Los Angeles, where she stayed until she retired in 1984. She now spends her time encouraging young people to enter the mathematics and science fields. She travels to schools as part of the Dow Chemical Company's Pioneers in Science program and also conducts math workshops for teachers, parents, and students.

I am most grateful for the fact that what I have been able to accomplish has inspired other women, particularly African American women, to pursue advanced studies in mathematics.

—Evelyn Boyd Granville

MARiE DALY

Triumph in Chemistry

SOMETIMES WOMEN LIVE out their parents' dreams. Marie Daly's father moved to the United States from the West Indies as a young man. He applied for and won a scholarship to Cornell University, hoping to study chemistry, but had to drop out after the first semester because he did not have enough money to pay his room and board. He became a postal clerk, married, and settled down in New York City to raise a family.

Young Marie, encouraged in her studies by both her parents, thought it would please her father if she became a scientist, since he could fulfill his own ambitions vicariously through her. Her high school teachers convinced her that she could be successful in chemistry. She attended Queens College in Flushing, New York, so that she could live at home and save money. Queens College was new and classes were small, an advantage in the lab courses Marie took. She graduated with honors in 1942.

Recognizing Marie's talent as well as the fact that she did not have the money for graduate school—a necessity for a professional chemist—the faculty of the chemistry department at Queens College gave her a fellowship and a part-time job as a laboratory assistant. With this help, she was able to enroll at New York University, where she finished her master's degree in one year. She worked at Queens College for another year, saving

enough money to enroll in the doctoral program at Columbia
University. She eventually received funds from the university that
enabled her to study full-time. She received her doctoral degree in
1947, becoming the first African American woman to receive a
Ph.D. in chemistry in the United States.

At this time the Rockefeller Institute, now Rockefeller University, was establishing its reputation as an important center for research. Marie was accepted there as a research apprentice, but had to raise her own research funds. Upon receiving a grant from the American Cancer Society in 1948, she worked at the Rockefeller Institute for seven years, focusing on the ways proteins are constructed within the cells of the body. In 1955 she moved to the College of Physicians and Surgeons at Columbia University, working on the underlying causes of heart attacks. With Dr. Quentin B. Deming, Marie discovered the part cholesterol plays in heart problems and also studied the effects of sugar and smoking on the heart.

In the 1960s, she and Dr. Deming moved their research project from Columbia University to Albert Einstein College of Medicine at Yeshiva University in New York City. At Yeshiva, she taught biochemistry while continuing her research, now working on the breakdown of the circulatory system caused by old age or hypertension. Marie also worked to increase minority enrollment in medical schools and science courses. She started a scholarship fund in physics or chemistry for minority students at Queens College in memory of her father, whose thwarted ambitions had been the catalyst for her own success. Marie retired in 1986.

CHRiSTINE DARDeN

Computer Genius

CHRISTINE DARDEN grew up in Monroe, North Carolina, the youngest of five children in a well-to-do family. Her father worked for an insurance company, and her mother was a teacher who started taking Christine to school with her when she was three. When Christine was four, she started kindergarten. She was a curious child and would take things apart to see how they worked. Her father encouraged her, teaching her basic car maintenance and repair. She also loved sports, especially baseball and roller skating.

She spent the last two years of high school at a small, private, all-girls college-preparatory school in Asheville, North Carolina. Here, her interest in mathematics bloomed. At the age of fifteen she was admitted to the Hampton Institute in Hampton, Virginia, and majored in education while continuing to study mathematics.

After her graduation from Hampton she taught junior high school and took night classes at Virginia State College. Believing that she could have a career in her chosen field of mathematics, she returned to school full-time at Virginia State, graduating in 1967. She accepted a job at the National Aeronautics and Space Administration (NASA) and worked at Langley Research Center in Hampton, Virginia.

Most of what you obtain in life will be because of your discipline. Discipline is perhaps more important than ability.

—**Christine Darden**

Her first job was with a computer group at a time when computers were room-sized calculators. She was one of the first people to write computer programs for modern computers. She also continued her studies, taking doctoral-level courses in mathematics and engineering at George Washington University, the first integrated school she had attended. While working full-time at NASA and raising three children, she got her Ph.D. in engineering in 1983, when she was one of very few African American women in the field. She continues to work at NASA and has become one of the leading experts in sonic boom technology.

DOROtHY BROWN
▲▲▲▲▲▲▲▲▲▲▲▲▲▲▲▲▲▲▲▲▲
Fighting Doctor

FROM A YOUNG AGE, Dorothy Brown wanted to be a doctor. First she had to grow up—not an easy task, as it turned out. Shortly after her birth in Troy, New York, in 1919, she was placed in an orphanage by her mother. She did not meet her father until she was an adult. She remained in the orphanage, which was predominantly white, until her mother took her back when she was twelve. Because she and her mother were strangers, it was not a happy reunion. She ran away from home five times, returning to the orphanage each time.

When Dorothy was fifteen she ran away again. This time she was determined to get a high school education and enrolled herself in

> I want to so order my life that its impression, its impact, might always be positive and spiritually constructive.
>
> **—Dorothy Brown**

Troy High School. The principal of the school helped by finding foster parents for her. Her foster family was kind and supportive, teaching her their own Christian values.

In 1937 she successfully completed high school and earned a scholarship to Bennett College in Greensboro, North Carolina. This was her first trip to the segregated South. After a shaky period of adjustment, she settled in and graduated second in her class.

Brown had wanted to be a doctor ever since she had her tonsils removed at age five. The timing was good; World War II made it possible for more women to enter medical school. She started at Meharry Medical College in 1944 and earned her M.D. four years later. She interned at Harlem Hospital for a year and then did a five-year residency in surgery at Meharry and Hubbard Hospital. Brown had almost no support in her decision to become a surgeon but, despite the opposition, she was the first Black female surgeon to become a fellow of the American College of Surgeons. In 1957 she was appointed chief of surgery at Nashville's Riverside Hospital, a position she held until 1983.

Medicine wasn't the only area in which she was a pioneer. Brown was the first single woman in Tennessee to adopt a child. She wanted to help a child the same way her foster family had helped her, so in 1956 she legally adopted her daughter Lola, whom she named after her own foster mother.

In 1966, it became evident that redistricting would make it possible to elect a Black candidate to the Tennessee state legislature. Brown accepted the request to run, becoming the first Black woman to serve in that state's legislative body. She resigned her seat after she lost a battle to expand abortion rights, a move she felt would save the lives of many women. She returned full-time to her medical practice and to caring for her daughter. Brown continues to practice medicine and teach in Nashville.

SHiRLEY JACKSoN
Feisty Physicist

SHIRLEY JACKSON is a brilliant physicist who was the first Black woman to earn a Ph.D. from the Massachusetts Institute of Technology (MIT). Both of her parents were strong advocates of a good education while she was growing up, and they encouraged her evident gift for science. Her father helped her with her science projects in school, including one that involved collecting live bumblebees in jars.

Her success later in life was also fueled by the times she grew up in. The 1954 Supreme Court decision in *Brown v. Board of Education* ordered school integration. In October 1957 the Russians launched Sputnik, prompting national interest in the sciences. The government was interested in and supported talented young Americans in the sciences, no matter their gender or color.

Shirley's talent placed her in the accelerated math and science program in high school, where she was a straight-A student and class valedictorian. She entered MIT in 1964, one of forty-five women and only a few Blacks in the 900-member freshman class. Her life was a lonely one. The men were not supportive of the women in the program, and the white women refused to allow her in their study group.

Still, the social and emotional pressures did not affect her academic work. When Shirley graduated in 1968, she was given a fellowship so that she could pursue a Ph.D. in physics at MIT. James Young, the first full-time tenured Black professor in the physics department, directed her graduate work. She received her Ph.D. in 1973, becoming the first Black woman to receive a Ph.D. in any category at MIT. Not content to rest on her laurels, she was a strong advocate for civil rights. She actively petitioned MIT to admit more minorities and tutored in Roxbury, Boston's Black neighborhood.

Shirley continued her postdoctoral studies on elementary particles at the Fermi National Accelerator Laboratory in Batavia, Illinois, and the European Center for Nuclear Research in Geneva, Switzerland. In 1976 she started working at AT&T Bell Laboratories in Murray Hill, New Jersey, combining her interest in theoretical particle physics with her employer's interest in gas, films, and semiconductors. She met and married a fellow physicist there.

I had to work alone. . . . At some level you have to decide you will persist in what you're doing and that you won't let people beat you down.

—**Shirley Jackson**

In 1985, Shirley was appointed by the governor of New Jersey to the New Jersey Commission on Science and Technology. She also served on the committees of the National Academy of Sciences, the American Association

Marjorie Browne inherited her father's love of mathematics, earning her doctorate in mathematics in 1949, and becoming one of the first two Black women to do so. She went on to teach at North Carolina Central University (NCCU), where she remained for thirty years, twenty-five of them as the only person with a Ph.D. in mathematics in the department. The primary author of a proposal to IBM to fund the first electronic digital computer at NCCU, which was installed under her direction in 1960 and 1961, Marjorie also won a Ford Foundation fellowship and was a National Science Foundation Faculty Fellow. In the last years of her life she used her own money to aid gifted young people who could not have completed their education otherwise.

for the Advancement of Science, and the National Science Foundation. She worked at Bell Labs until 1991, when she became a professor of physics at Rutgers University in New Jersey. That year also marked one of Shirley's most treasured honors: she was elected to life membership on the board of trustees of MIT, where she had once been a lonely female minority student.

In 1995, she was nominated by President Clinton to the chairmanship of the Nuclear Regulatory Commission. She accepted the position at a time when great concern regarding nuclear energy was rampant. Shirley took on the challenge with her usual determination and proved to be a strong advocate for honesty and safety in the nuclear energy industry. In 1997 she led the formation of the International Nuclear Regulators Association and served as its first chairman until May 1999, when she resigned her position with the NRC and became the first Black woman president of Rensselaer Polytechnic Institute.

Shirley holds ten honorary degrees, received the New Jersey Governor's Award in Science in 1993, and was inducted into the National Women's Hall of Fame in 1998.

FLEMMiE KITTRELL

▲▲▲▲▲▲▲▲▲▲▲▲▲▲▲▲▲▲▲▲▲▲▲▲▲▲▲▲

International Home Economist

FLEMMIE KITTRELL was destined to turn an interest in home economics into an international career. She was born on Christmas Day 1904 in Henderson, North Carolina, the seventh of nine children and the youngest girl. Home life was happy; her father made it a point to praise his children for their accomplishments and her mother was her closest friend. At home, she developed the traits that would keep her in good stead later in life: to set goals, take action, and not give up until her goals were achieved.

Flemmie graduated from high school with honors and then attended Hampton Institute in Virginia, receiving a bachelor of science degree in 1928 with majors in home economics and general science. She took a teaching position at Bennett College in Greensboro, North Carolina.

Her teachers had encouraged her to go to graduate school in home economics at Cornell University in Ithaca, New York, the best program of its kind in the country. At first Kittrell resisted because she thought she would feel out of place in the North, but eventually she relented, not least of all because she was awarded a scholarship. The only graduate program she could enter at Cornell, however, was in nutrition, the field of home economics she liked least.

When she arrived at Cornell and went to register for a room, Kittrell was told that she would have to find housing off-campus. She immediately went to the university president, who gave her a letter to take to the dean of women, securing her a place in the women's dormitory. After she received her Ph.D., she returned to Bennett College but was soon offered a job at Hampton Institute as head of the home economics department and dean of women.

Although the place of home economics in a university was controversial, Kittrell saw it as a field of research where results could lead to solutions to practical problems. Both research programs and outreach services were the cornerstones of her career.

In 1944 she accepted a position on the faculty of Howard University in Washington, D.C., after the school promised to build a new building exclusively for home economics. It took twenty years for them to fulfill that promise. Meanwhile, Kittrell built an international reputation in her field. One of her most important contributions at Howard was the establishment of a nursery school program that served both as a training site and a laboratory for research in human development. Her studies there laid the foundation for the Head Start program of the 1960s.

In 1946 the United States Department of State asked her to lead a field survey of nutritional practices and needs in Liberia. The six-month project revealed hidden hunger, a condition in which people have enough to eat but are nevertheless severely malnourished, and she established a program that helped the Liberians keep a more balanced diet.

In 1950 the State Department requested her help on a project in India to create a college-level training program for home economists. In August 1953 Kittrell returned to India as a Fulbright Scholar and participated in the first graduation ceremonies at the school she helped establish. Internationally known, she was in demand as a lecturer in Africa, Southeast Asia, and Pacific Rim countries. While the Cold War was at its height, the Soviet Union invited her to tour Russia. In 1962, after the Belgian Congo won independence, she was invited by Methodist missionaries to help establish schools there. Kittrell also designed a program for Howard University to facilitate recruitment of international students. As a result of her work, Howard University became known worldwide for its home economics programs.

ANGELA FERGUSON

Relentless Researcher

Despite the fact that Angela Ferguson's father was a teacher and an accomplished architect, his family suffered from poverty. It was the Great Depression of the 1930s, and money was difficult to come by no matter what your skills. Angela worked in the school cafeteria while she was in grade school to earn her lunches. Meals

at home often consisted of boiled potatoes. There was no water
when the bill could not be paid.

During her second year of high school, Angela took the required science courses and became fascinated with chemistry, an interest she carried into her first year at Howard University. Her parents had managed to save enough for her first year's tuition, and after that she continued on scholarships and what she could earn working summers at Freedmen's Hospital. Biology caught her interest in her second year. Before long she had decided to become both a scientist and a medical doctor.

Angela entered medical school at Howard and became fascinated with pediatrics. After earning her medical degree in 1949, she interned in general medicine at Freedmen's Hospital, then completed her residency in pediatrics. After graduation she opened a private practice in pediatrics.

Up until this time, all of the research done in developmental physiology had been based on white children. Seeing the need for research on African American children, Ferguson joined the staff of the Howard University School of Medicine as a research associate. During her work there, she realized that a great many African American children suffered from sickle-cell anemia, a hereditary disease that causes the red blood cells to take on the shape of a sickle and to interfere with blood flow. This can cause pain and swelling, and even stroke or death.

Since the early symptoms mimic other conditions, the disease was often not diagnosed correctly at an early age. Ferguson made a study of hundreds of sickle-cell patients and discovered the early symptoms, which were published and distributed to doctors

121

all over the country. She then concentrated on better treatments for the disease. The most important change she instituted was the practice of giving newborn African American babies a blood test so that the disease could be detected as early as possible.

In the 1960s, Ferguson moved from research to administrative work. In 1970 she took over administration of the University Office of Health Affairs, which oversees all facility development, student health services, research, and advanced instruction for all degree programs at Howard Medical School. In 1979 Ferguson be-

GERTRUDE ABOAGYE: ANIMAL SPECIALIST

Gertrude Aboagye has devoted her life to helping her native country, Ghana, and the rest of the world improve the productivity of their livestock. Born in Accra, Ghana, in 1947, Gertrude studied agriculture at the University of Ghana, and then earned a master's degree in animal breeding at the University of Guelph in Ontario, Canada. After completing her education, she moved back to Ghana in 1976, where she became a teacher in the Department of Animal Science at the University of Ghana. Her specialty is cattle production and animal breeding, which she teaches to undergraduate students. In addition to her teaching duties, Gertrude works with the Animal Breeding Consultant Team in Ghana, funded by the World Bank, and also with the Animal Genetics Resources Group, which is run by the Food and Agriculture Organization (FAO) of the United Nations. The Animal Genetics Resources Group is developing the Domestic Animal Diversity Information System (DAD-IS) as part of the FAO's Global Program, which aims to help countries implement national strategies for managing their animal genetic resources in order to improve the productivity of their livestock. Gertrude works on the Breeds database in DAD-IS. Her work is improving the future for her country and the rest of us as well.

came the university's associate vice president for health affairs, a position she held until her retirement in 1990. Because of her pioneering work, sickle-cell disease can now be detected and controlled much more efficiently.

JEWELL COBB
▲▲▲▲▲▲▲▲▲▲▲▲▲▲▲▲▲▲▲▲

Cancer Researcher

JEWELL COBB grew up in a family that valued education. Her grandfather was a pharmacist, her father a medical doctor. Her mother had studied dance at Sargents College, associated with Harvard University, and taught dance in the Chicago public schools. Jewell was encouraged to read about politics, current events, and scientific discoveries. The family often attended ballets and musicals. When Jewell entered college, her mother decided to return also. They both received degrees in 1944.

In high school, Jewell had decided to become a biologist. She chose to continue her education at the University of Michigan, but the dormitories were still segregated at that time, and the climate of a large institution did not agree with her. She transferred to Talladega College in Talladega, Alabama, completing her college work in three years.

Jewell was then accepted to New York University graduate school, although they did not offer her the teaching fellowship she had hoped for. Undeterred, Jewell went to New York City and talked to the university officials in person. They were so impressed that they awarded her a teaching fellowship for the entire five years of her graduate studies, during which she studied cell growth. She began work on her Ph.D. in 1947, and in 1949 spent a summer doing research at the Marine Biological Laboratory in Woods Hole, Massachusetts. After completing her doctorate in cell physiology in 1950, she was awarded a post-doctoral fellowship by the National Cancer Institute, and spent two years doing research on cell growth and studying anti-cancer chemicals.

Jewell took a short hiatus in the late '50s, marrying Roy Cobb in 1954 and giving birth to their son Jonathan in 1957. She returned to New York University, teaching courses in biology, renewing her research on skin cells, and supervising the research done in her lab until 1960, when she became professor of biology at Sarah Lawrence College in Bronxville, New York. In 1969 she moved to Connecticut College in New London, Connecticut, where she not only was professor of zoology but was director of the cell biology laboratory and dean of the college. In 1976 she transferred to Douglass College, a branch of Rutgers University, in New Brunswick, New Jersey, where she was named dean and professor of biological science.

That same year Jewell began a campaign to increase the number of women

Jewell Cobb

and minorities in science and engineering. That campaign resulted in her appointment as president of the California State University in Fullerton, California, in 1981. During her tenure, she increased the diversity of the student body and strengthened support for the university's engineering and science programs. A new multiethnic residence hall was built and named in her honor.

By the time of her retirement, Jewell's research had helped others scientists understand how the skin is affected by ultraviolet radiation, and we now know that too much sun can be harmful to the skin and cause skin cancer. She wrote more than thirty-six research articles and tested many chemicals for the treatment of skin cancer. Ten institutions of higher education have awarded Jewell honorary degrees, and she has been sent to England, Russia, and Italy by U.S. government agencies to study and teach.

The family tradition of excellence in science is being carried on by her son Jonathan, who is a medical doctor and is doing research on radiation.

MAE JEMISON
▲▲▲▲▲▲▲▲▲▲▲▲▲▲▲▲▲▲▲▲▲▲▲▲▲▲

Black Astronaut

MAE WANTED TO go where no woman had gone before—and she finally made it. She was raised in Chicago and graduated from high school in 1973. She went on to earn a B.S. in chemical engineering at Stanford University, having won a National

Achievements Scholarship, and concurrently earned a B.A. in African American Studies. Next she attended medical school at Cornell University, where she received an M.D. in 1981. While she was in medical school, she traveled to Cuba, Kenya, and Thailand, providing medical care to indigent people. She completed her internship at the University of Southern California Medical Center in Los Angeles, then served in the Peace Corps in Sierra Leone and Liberia from 1983 to 1985.

When Mae returned to the United States, she went to work for the CIGNA Health Plans of California, practicing general medicine in Los Angeles while attending graduate classes in engineering. She applied to the National Aeronautics and Space Administration (NASA) for the astronaut program but was turned down. Her second application in 1987 was accepted, one of fifteen chosen from 2,000 applicants. She completed her training in August 1988, becoming the first Black female astronaut in NASA history. In August 1992 she became the first Black woman in space. When she went into space, she took a poster depicting the dance "Cry," the signature piece of Judith Jamison, who is the director of the Alvin Ailey American Dance Theater. Mae believed that the dance was created for Jamison and "all Black women everywhere."

> Science is very important to me, but I also like to stress that you have to be well-rounded. . . . I truly feel someone interested in science is interested in understanding what's going on in the world.
>
> **—Mae Jemison**

Mae is based at NASA's Lyndon B. Johnson Space Center in Houston, Texas, where she is an outspoken advocate for African Americans in science and engineering.

CAROLYN BROOKS

▲▲▲▲▲▲▲▲▲▲▲▲▲▲▲▲▲▲▲▲▲▲

Finding the Magic in Beans

CAROLYN BROOKS grew up in an extended family in post-World War II Richmond, Virginia. While her parents worked, she was cared for by her great-grandparents and her older sister. Her parents worked hard to provide for her and her sister. In return, Carolyn excelled at school and in sports.

When the walls of segregation tumbled in Richmond, Carolyn preferred to continue to attend her old school, where she felt supported by teachers and friends. One of the benefits of the newly liberal atmosphere, however, was the establishment of a special summer program geared to interest minority students in careers in science. There, Carolyn heard a medical microbiologist speak and decided this was the field for her.

She was offered scholarships to six colleges, and she decided on Tuskegee University partly because it would allow her to travel to a different part of the country. There, she majored in biology and briefly considered medical school. Fearing that she wouldn't be able to handle losing a patient, she decided to stick to microbiology. At the end of her second year, she married and considered giving up college to focus on her family, but her husband and professors encouraged her to continue. Carolyn received her bachelor's degree in 1968, while raising two sons. In 1971 she earned her master's degree, having also added a daughter to the family.

After she had worked for a short time at the local Veteran's Administration hospital, her husband was accepted into a doctoral program at Ohio State University. Carolyn applied to the department of microbiology at Ohio State and was not only accepted but given a fellowship to boot.

Moving from Tuskegee, a traditionally Black institution, to Ohio State was a shock. There were no Blacks on the faculty and very few Black students in her department. Her lab partner was convinced she was there only because of affirmative action. Carolyn adjusted, concentrating on her work on T-cells, and received her doctoral degree in 1977.

At her first job, Carolyn focused on the nutritional needs of the elderly. A few years later, she began to do studies on the relationship between microbes and legumes, researching ways to increase the productivity of certain microbes that in turn increase the nutritive value of the plant. Her research has led her to spend time in Togo, Senegal, and Cameroon in West Africa, studying the legumes there. She has also worked on genetic engineering, trying to make plants more insect resistant.

Carolyn has received numerous awards for her research, but those that are most important to her have recognized her community service and her abilities as a mentor to her students.

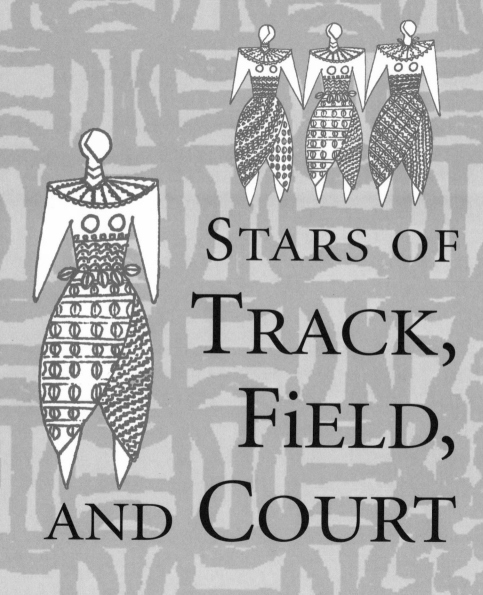

Stars of Track, Field, and Court

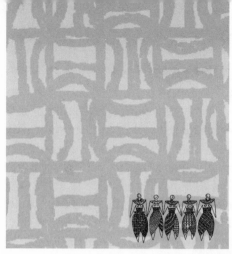

ANA FIDELiA QUIROT

Heroic Runner

AS A YOUNG GIRL growing up in a small village in eastern Cuba in the 1960s, Ana Quirot was happy but somewhat less than studious. She was misdiagnosed with learning disabilities and sent to a special education school, which turned out to be a blessing in disguise. There, a coach saw her racing and recognized her potential. At ten she set a record at a sports meet in Santiago de Cuba, even though she was running barefoot, and at twelve she was showing her talents in the long jump. Cuba had established a nationwide system of Sports Initiation Schools to assist young athletes. Ana was enrolled in one of these schools and had a promising future in sports ahead of her.

But then her adolescent body betrayed her. Her speed and agility suddenly disappeared. She was short and she became overweight.

Over time, she stopped practicing as hard as she should have. When Ana was told she was being dropped from the sports school, she thought her world was ending. Fortunately for her, Blas Beato, a veteran trainer, had seen her and thought she had potential for the 400 meter. Under his guidance, she lost her excess pounds, built up her endurance, and gained self-confidence. She became unbeatable and as a member of Cuba's national track and field team she was soon setting national records in both the 400 and 800 meters. In 1987, the world took note when she won two gold medals at the Pan Am Games in Indianapolis. The next year Cuba boycotted the Seoul Olympics, but Ana never mourned the medals that would have been hers. Instead she graduated magna cum laude from college with a degree in physical culture and met and married Raul Cascaret, a world-champion wrestler. They were divorced in 1991 but remained friends until his death in a car accident.

After winning the Gran Premio International in Track and Field in 1987, 1988, and 1989, Ana was crowned the world's Best Woman Athlete in 1989. 1992, an Olympic year, brought setbacks. She suffered her first leg injury, causing concern for her performance in the Olympics. Two months before the games started, her coach and dear friend Blas Beato died of cancer. And she was pregnant. This slowed her down enough that she only took the bronze medal in the 800 meters.

After the Olympics, Ana decided to take some time off to have her baby, who had been fathered by Javier Sotomayor, a world-record high jumper. Tests had shown it was a girl, and Ana had all the dreams for her daughter that any mother would have. Near the end of her pregnancy, in January 1993, Ana was boiling diapers for the baby's layette. Because of the shortage of soap and bleach caused by the U.S. embargo, Cubans added a few drops of alcohol to clothes to whiten them as they boiled them over a kerosene stove. The bottle of alcohol in Ana's hand caught fire and ignited her clothes. When she tried to pull her sweater off, it stuck to her upper body. That night she was rushed to the hospital with third-degree burns over 10 percent of her body and second-degree burns over another 30 percent. All of Cuba tuned in for the medical bulletins while friends, teammates, reporters, and even Castro rushed to her bedside.

Ana Fidelia Quirot

The doctors weren't certain she would live and, if she did, they were certain she would never move normally again, let alone run. Labor was induced; the child died after ten days on life support. The doctors didn't tell Ana until later because they were afraid she would give up fighting for her own life. Ana spent five months in the hospital and several more having restorative surgeries. In one year, she had twenty-one surgeries.

To maximize the potential of her returning to racing, the doctors took skin grafts from her back rather than her legs and also used synthetic human skin.

As soon as she could, Ana began running up and down the fifteen flights of stairs in the hospital to get in shape. All of the agony was worth it when she removed her bandages and ran five laps around the track. "People told me they didn't understand how I could do it, how I could overcome all those difficulties. But if I did not run again, I would have died." Ana credits her remarkable recovery to the support of her family and friends and to the visit from Fidel Castro, for who she is named.

Although the burns have limited the movement of her arms and head, they have not affected her lower body. In the fall of 1993, Ana insisted on running in the Central American and Caribbean games in Puerto Rico. She took a silver medal, even though she still could not swing her arms. Back in Cuba, at the welcoming ceremonies for Cuba's athletes, Castro said, "She won the silver medal in the race, but a great gold medal for willpower." She returned to international competition in 1995, winning the gold medal in the 800 meters in the World Championship at Goteberg, Sweden. At the 1996 Olympics, she took a silver medal, and she earned a gold medal in the 1997 World Championships in Athens.

MARiA MUTOLA

Don't Stop Running

ONE OF ANA QUIROT's fiercest competitors has been Maria Mutola, whose swift feet have carried her from war-torn Mozambique to international fame.

Growing up in Maputo, the capital of Mozambique, Maria played soccer in the streets and wondered what it would be like to live in a country without warfare. Mozambique had been in the midst of a bloody civil war since 1975. It wasn't until 1993, when the civil war had ended, that she was able to safely travel around the country. Due to her athletic prowess, however, she traveled much farther before that.

At fourteen she was the only girl on her soccer team. When she scored the winning goal in a league championship game, the opposing team said it wasn't fair for a girl to play. League officials agreed and awarded the opposing team the title. A prominent Mozambican poet, Jose Craveirinha, saw a story about the incident in the newspaper. He contacted Maria and introduced her to his son, a track and field coach, who gave her a pair of training shoes and coached her for seven days in distance running. By the seventh day she was so sore she quit, and stayed away for a week. Having been told by his son that she had quit, Jose went to visit her family, convincing them that she had a future in track. Soon she was back running. Only a few months later she represented her country at the 1988 Olympics, taking seventh in the 800-meter race.

Maria's showing in the Olympics brought her to the attention of Olympic Solidarity, a group that helps promising Third World athletes train in other countries. They awarded her a scholarship and she came to Eugene, Oregon, to train and attend high school. Her high school counselor, who spoke Portuguese, her native tongue, helped find her a family to live with. They learned to enjoy Mozambican foods and she learned to laugh at movies she didn't understand.

She had been excited about coming to the United States but the transition was difficult. Marie spoke no English and she was one of the few minority students in her school. She was far from home in the middle of a culture she didn't understand. She wanted to go home. Her sister convinced her to stay, for which Maria was later grateful. Two months after she arrived, she broke the Mozambique record for the 1,500 meters in the Oregon Invitational.

But there were disappointments. She placed fifth in the 800 at the 1992 Olympics and was disqualified in the Worlds in 1995 when she stepped out of her lane in her semifinal race. A little failure has not stopped her. She took the gold at the 1993 Worlds, the bronze in the 800 at the 1996 Olympics, and broke the ten-year-old world indoor record in the 800 in February 1998. Already a champion in the 800, she is working at becoming one in the 1,500 also.

She now earns $250,000 a year, owns her own home, and faithfully sends money to her family in Mozambique. Maria has brought her niece, who also wants to be a runner, to live with her because she wants to pass on the help she received.

Maria visits Mozambique every year, where she is an idol. People call her by name, children follow her in the streets, and she visits with the president. The little girl who played soccer in the dirt-covered streets has come a long way on her winged feet.

TONI STONE

▲▲▲▲▲▲▲▲▲▲▲▲▲▲▲▲▲▲▲▲▲

Talented Tomboy

THE NEGRO LEAGUES were founded in 1920. The next year Maracenia Lyle was born. Under the name Toni Stone, her life-long interest in baseball would eventually lead her to be one of the few woman players in Negro baseball.

As a child, she was definitely a tomboy. "I loved my trousers, my jeans. I loved cars. Most of all I loved to ride horses with no saddles," she once said. "I wasn't classified. People weren't ready for me." Despite the fact that a woman's involvement in baseball was not acceptable in polite society, Stone was determined to play. Her parents didn't understand their daughter's interest in base-ball, but they supported her nonetheless. When she was ten, she began to play in what was the Little League of the day. Later she played for a girls' softball club in St. Paul, Minnesota. At fifteen she joined a semi-professional men's team, the St. Paul Giants.

Stone eventually pressured the minor league St. Paul Saints' team manager into letting her try out for the team. He was so im-pressed with her abilities that he invited her to his baseball camp. After high school Stone played with several semi-pro teams in her hometown area. During World War II, she joined her sister in

A woman has her dreams, too. When you finish high school, they tell a boy to go out and see the world. What do they tell a girl? They tell her to go next door and marry the boy that their family's picked out for her. It wasn't right.

—**Toni Stone**

Oakland, California. Apparently she arrived with less than a dollar in her pocket, found a job, a place to live, and a baseball team to play on before she even found her sister.

At first, she played centerfield for Al Love's American Legion team, but soon joined the San Francisco Sea Lions, a barnstorming team that toured the South. She batted .280 and was on the Negro League's All Star team. Stone did not get to play as much as she had been promised she would, so she left the Sea Lions for the New Orleans Black Pelicans.

During the off-season, she returned to Oakland, where she met and married Aurelious Alberga, a man forty years her senior and a first lieutenant in the Officer Reserves Corps. He didn't want Stone to keep playing baseball, but obviously he didn't know who he was dealing with, because she continued undaunted.

In 1949, Stone began playing second base for the New Orleans Creoles, a minor league team. Four years later, the Negro Leagues were in serious trouble. National League baseball had been integrated in 1947 by the success of Jackie Robinson, and all of the best Black players were now being recruited into integrated ball. To gain the team some attention, Stone was hired by the owner of the Indianapolis Clowns. She was now a well-seasoned thirty-two-year-old player. During her stint with the Clowns, she experienced one of the highlights of her career, a hit off the legendary pitcher Satchel Paige. "That was the finest thing to happen to me in my life," she remembered. "He threw that fastball and I didn't go nowhere, just stood up there and hit it across second base. And I was so tickled to death I was laughing all the way to first base, and started to round first base and fell. . . . I laughed like hell, and he was laughing, too."

She played fifty games for the Clowns, mostly exhibition games, maintaining a .243 batting average. In 1953 she was traded to the Kansas City Monarchs. She did not get to play much and retired at the end of that season. She returned to Oakland, finding work as a nurse and taking care of her husband until he died in 1987 at the age of 103. True to her love of the sport, she also continued to play sandlot and pickup games with the California American Legion until she was sixty-two. She was inducted into the International Women's Sports Hall of Fame in 1985. March 6, 1990 was proclaimed "Toni Stone Day" in her hometown of St. Paul, and in 1992, the Baseball Hall of Fame in Cooperstown, New York, recognized her contributions to baseball, along with seventy-two male players from the Negro Leagues. She died of heart failure in 1996.

WiLLYE WHiTE
▲▲▲▲▲▲▲▲▲▲▲▲▲▲▲▲▲▲
Five-Time Olympic Athlete

WILLYE WHITE was a natural athlete and competed in the Olympics for more years than any other female. She was born New Year's Day 1940 in Money, Mississippi. She grew up in

As a child in Griffin, Georgia, Wyomia Tyus suffered from polio. She wore corrective shoes until she was ten years old. Eight years later she took gold at the 1964 Tokyo Olympics, running the 100-meter dash. At the Mexico City Olympics in 1968, she became one of only two women who, up until that time, had ever won three gold medals, a feat that placed her in the Olympic Hall of Fame.

Greenwood, Mississippi, and was raised by her grandparents. Later they moved to Chicago. Her athletic abilities became evident in grade school; while she was in the fifth grade, she was playing on the high school varsity basketball team.

Willye was invited to attend Tennessee State University's summer clinic for potential Olympic contenders, and spent four summers there, competing in her first Olympics in 1956 at the age of sixteen. She returned to Chicago and completed high school, where she was in the band, in the choir, and on the basketball team. She went on to compete in the 1960, 1964, 1968, and 1972 games, winning the silver medal for the long jump in 1956 and 1964. During her athletic career, she was a member of thirty-nine international teams, including four Pan American teams and five Olympic teams; she was also the holder of the American long jump record for sixteen years.

She spent a year at Tennessee State University on a track scholarship, but left after a year to go into nursing. Realizing that her intense participation in athletics might interfere with obtaining a nursing degree, she became a practical nurse instead. Her participation in Olympic competition complete, she returned to college and received a B.A. in public health care administration in 1976, along with a coaching certificate.

Willye has been inducted into the National Track and Field Hall of Fame as well as the Black Athletes Hall of Fame, has served on the President's Commission on Olympic Sports, and was president of the Illinois Amateur Athletic Union from 1980 to 1986.

Working for the Chicago Health Department, Willye has been a volunteer coach for local track clubs, eventually becoming the director of recreation services for the Chicago Park Districts, where she fights for more and better programs for young Black athletes.

ALiCE COAChMAN
▲▲▲▲▲▲▲▲▲▲▲▲▲▲▲▲▲▲▲▲▲▲▲▲
High Jumper Extraordinaire

ALICE COACHMAN used her athletic abilities to jump her way into the history books, both as a world-class athlete and as the first Black woman hired to endorse an international product, Coca-Cola.

While growing up in Albany, Georgia, Alice would tie rags together and string them between trees in order to practice high jumping. Her father, wanting his daughters to be models of femininity (translation: cooking, cleaning, and taking care of a man) had no patience with her interest in athletics and would beat her whenever she would go out to run or jump.

Alice kept it up anyway and was rewarded when she broke the AAU high school and college women's high jump records (barefoot) and received a working scholarship to Tuskegee Institute.

At the 1948 London Olympics, Mickey Patterson-Tyler became the first U.S. woman to run the new 220-yard dash. She took a bronze medal in the event, becoming the first Black woman to win an Olympic medal. (The only other American woman to win a medal in that Olympics was Alice Coachman.) In the mid-1960s she married and settled in San Diego, where she began coaching children, and founded Mickey's Missiles, a national track team made up of young people from all racial, economic, and social backgrounds, and an attempt to promote racial harmony through sports. Her efforts touched the lives of more than 5,000 children.

Alice Coachman

While there, she won twenty-six national titles in the high jump and the 50-meter dash. She also played soccer, field hockey, volleyball, and basketball. Alice didn't spend all of her time on the field, however. She sang in the school choir and performed with the drill team, while working her way through school by cleaning the pool and gym and rolling the clay tennis courts.

The Olympic Games were cancelled in 1940 and 1944 because of World War II, so Coachman did not make an appearance until 1948, when, at age twenty-four, she was thought to be past her prime. She watched her teammates lose one by one, until it was her turn. She took the gold in the high jump, becoming the first Black woman to win an Olympic gold medal.

When she returned to the United States after the games, she was rewarded with an invitation to the White House, a victory motorcade through her home state of Georgia, and a contract to endorse Coca-Cola.

Coachman became a coach and teacher and was inducted into the National Track and Field Hall of Fame in 1975. After she retired, she founded the Alice Coachman Track and Field Foundation to help children and retired athletes.

ZiNA GARRISON
Queen of the Court

AT THE AGE of ten, Zina Garrison began playing tennis on local public courts. The coach was impressed with her abilities and entered her in local tournaments. At sixteen, she was playing in national tournaments. She won the 1979 National Hard Court Doubles Championship for sixteen and under and the 1980 National Girls Sixteen Singles Championship. In 1981, Zina was the first Black player to win the junior singles championship at Wimbledon, also winning the junior singles titles at the U.S. Open that year. The U.S. Olympic Committee named her the top female amateur athlete in tennis, and the next year she turned pro with a ranking of sixteenth in the world.

> And my goal now is to widen the opportunity for a better citizenry.
>
> —**Zina Garrison**

She was a member of the 1988 U.S. Olympic tennis team, the first U.S. tennis team to compete in the Olympics since 1924.

She was the singles runner-up at Wimbledon in 1990, defeating both Monica Seles and Steffi Graf. She was the first Black woman to reach the singles final of the Grand Slam tournament since Althea Gibson in 1958. At the 1992 Olympic games, she took the gold medal in doubles and a bronze in singles. Among the highlights of her career was her defeat of Chris Evert during the last tournament of Evert's career.

During her career, Zina won many championships and millions of dollars in prize money. She was ranked among the top ten women tennis players in the world from 1983 to 1991 and was the number one Black player. A mark of her character, both on and off the court, was that she was one of the few players known for applauding a good shot by her opponent.

Following her retirement in 1997, she opened the Zina Garrison All Court Tennis Academy, dedicated to promoting self-esteem among minority children through tennis. She is also head of the Zina Garrison Foundation, providing funds and support for the homeless, youth organizations, and anti-drug groups.

FLORA "FLO" HYMAN

▲▲▲▲▲▲▲▲▲▲▲▲▲▲▲▲▲▲▲▲▲▲▲▲▲

Volleyball Star

FLORA HYMAN began playing volleyball as a teenager in Inglewood, California, during the mid-1950s. Before her career was cut short, she was considered to be the best player in the history of the U.S. women's volleyball program. After studying math and physical education at the University of Houston for three years, being named the outstanding collegiate player of 1976, and being a three-time All American, Flo decided to follow her volleyball dreams. She moved to Colorado to join the national program.

At 6 feet 5 inches, Flo was famous for her spiking ability and her defensive skills. She was equally famous for her personal integrity and charisma. She was on the U.S. team for the World Cup tournaments in 1977 and 1981 and for the world championships in 1978 and 1982. In 1983 she and her coach accepted the Team of the Year Award from the Women's Sports Foundation.

After the U.S. team won the silver medal in the 1984 Los Angeles Olympics, she went to Japan to play for a semi-professional team sponsored by a Japanese supermarket chain. In no time at all, she was a star in her adopted

I had to learn to be honest with myself. I had to recognize my pain threshold. When I hit the floor, I have to realize it's not as if I broke a bone. Pushing yourself over the barrier is a habit. . . . If you want to win the war, you've got to pay the price.

—Flo Hyman

country, but in 1986, at the height of her abilities, she collapsed and died of heart failure during a game. The autopsy revealed that she had suffered from an undiagnosed case of Marfan's Syndrome, a congenital defect of the heart that affects tall, thin people. The Flo Hyman Memorial Award is given annually by the Women's Sports Foundation to a female athlete who embodies Hyman's "dignity, spirit, and commitment to excellence."

LUiSA HARRiS-STEWART

Hoop Queen

WHEN LUISA HARRIS-STEWART was a little girl, she dreamed of being a basketball star even though at the time there were no professional women's basketball teams. The seventh of nine children, she was born in 1955 in Minter City, Mississippi. She grew up playing basketball, first with her brothers and sisters at home, and then on the courts of her junior and senior high schools. She was recruited by a small white college in Cleveland, Mississippi, and led her team to three Association of Intercollegiate Athletics for Women (AIAW) basketball championships in 1975, 1976, and 1977.

The 6-foot 3-inch center dominated women's basketball in the mid-1970s. Luisa was high scorer at the 1976 Olympics, the first time women's basketball was an Olympic sport, leading her team as they took the silver medal. In 1976 she was voted most valuable player at the AIAW national championship and also proclaimed Mississippi's first Amateur Athlete of the Year. In 1977 she won the Broderick Award for the top basketball player in the AIAW and the Broderick Cup for outstanding female collegiate athlete.

At the time Luisa won all of these awards, she was attending school full-time and was a leader on campus. In addition to her feats as an athlete, she was the first Black woman at Delta State University to be chosen homecoming queen.

Unfortunately, there was nowhere for her to go after college, at least nothing comparable to the men's leagues. She played for a time in the short-lived Women's Pro League in 1980. She ultimately married, had four sons, and now teaches physical education and coaches women's basketball. Luisa was one of the first two women inducted into the Springfield Basketball Hall of Fame in May 1992.

OTHER SPORTS STARS

- Although she was born with polio and unable to walk well until she was ten, Wilma Rudolph was the first woman to win three track gold medals in the 1960 Olympics.
- In 1956, Althea Gibson became the first Black to win a major tennis title when she won the women's singles in the French Open.
- Renee Powell became the first Black woman on the Ladies' Professional Golf Association (LPGA) tour in 1967.
- The first Black ice skater on a World Team was Debi Thomas in 1984. She went on to win the silver medal in the 1988 Winter Olympics, becoming the first Black athlete to take a medal in the Winter Olympics.

Sassy Songbirds, Dazzling Dancers, and Talented Thespians

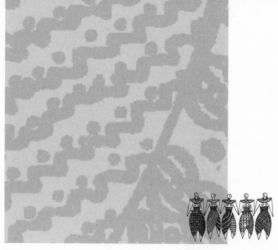

OUMOU SANGARE

A Voice for Freedom

O UMOU SANGARE uses her mellifluous voice to express her concern about the condition of women in her country. She was born in Bamako, Mali, a landlocked country in western Africa, in 1968. Her parents had moved there from the area in Mali known as Wassoulou, south of the Niger River. Her mother, also a singer, was one of three wives, and Oumou saw firsthand the suffering polygamy could bring.

Oumou started singing in public when she was six. Later she became a member of the National Ensemble of Mali, where many of her country's top musicians had been trained. In 1986 she joined the percussion troupe Djoliba for a tour of Europe, and returned home determined to form her own group grounded in the musical traditions of Wassoulou, her ancestral homeland. She began to work with arranger Amadou Ba Guindo and a group of musicians. After two years of work they recorded their first album, *Mousolou* ("Women"), which sold more than 200,000 copies in West Africa. At age twenty-one Oumou was a star.

Wassoulou music offers an alternative to the predominant music of Mali known as the Jalis, which are sung in praise of important men and the glory of the ancestors. In contrast, Wassoulou singers sing of everyday concerns. While Jali audiences are expected to sit in quiet reverence, Wassoulou audiences are invited to get up and dance to the music.

Oumou uses her music to expose the problems women suffer in male-dominated Muslim societies such as hers, attacking polygamy, female circumcision, arranged marriages, and the idea that women should be subject to men. Islam is the dominant religion all of the countries of the northern half of the African continent and is influential along the eastern seaboard as well. Her songs are helping to make a difference. But she also sings beautiful love songs. Her voice has been compared to that of Aretha Franklin in its soaring soulfulness.

Living out her beliefs, she chose her own husband—a radical act in Mali—and has followed her own choice of career. But lest anyone should think she is anti-male, she has said, "I'm not against men, I adore them all. But we want to defend the rights of women."

QUEEN LATiFAh

▲▲▲▲▲▲▲▲▲▲▲▲▲▲▲▲▲▲▲▲▲▲▲▲

Quadruple-Threat Artist

QUEEN LATIFAH is a multitalented artist who has made her mark in music, acting, artist management, and now as a talk show host. Born Dana Owens in Newark, New Jersey, in 1970, she is the daughter of a retired police officer and an art teacher. The Queen's stage name derives from a nickname given to her by a Muslim cousin. *Latifah* means "feminine, nice, and kind" in Arabic.

She began her career at eighteen, and her first CD, the Grammy-nominated *All Hail the Queen,* sold more than 1 million copies, making Queen Latifah one of the first successful women in the male-dominated field of rap music. In 1994 she won her first Grammy for Best Rap Solo Performance for her hit single, "U.N.I.T.Y." Her career expanded into acting when she landed a starring role in the television series *Living Single,* a role she played for five years. She went on to roles in the movies *Jungle Fever, Hoodlum, Sphere, My Life, Living Out Loud, The Bone Collector,* and a star turn in *Set It Off.* Her talent earned her the Spirit Award for Best Actress in 1996.

A savvy businesswoman who is committed to nurturing new talent, Queen Latifah established her own music label and artist management firm, Flavor Unit Entertainment. Her nationally syndicated daytime talk show debuted in September 1999.

> I think I was born independent. I had a compulsive heart to find out new things. They were sometimes things that endangered my life, but I had to discover the world.
>
> **—Queen Latifah**

Queen Latifah has not forgotten where she comes from and gives back generously to her community. When her brother Lance was killed in a motorcycle accident in 1993, she established the Lancelot H. Owens Foundation, which awards scholarships to academically gifted students with limited financial resources. She also donates money from her talk show that will be used by the public schools in her home town of Newark for job training and classes in the arts, and she generously contributes her time and money to many charities, especially those that support children and AIDS research.

CESARiA EVORA

The Barefoot Diva

MINDELO IS A port town with a busy nightlife on the Cape Verde island of São Vicente, off the coast of Senegal in Africa. All types of music are popular there, but the most popular styles are the *coladera* and the *morna*. The morna is a slow and rhythmic song-form that expresses nostalgia, love, sadness, and longing; it is often compared to the blues.

Because of her powerful voice, full of vulnerability and emotion, Cesaria Evora quickly established herself as the "Queen of Morna." She and her band began performing in Mindelo when she was in her teens, going from club to club, depending on the generosity of their fans to make a living. But trade in Mindelo began to decline in the late 1950s. Many musicians, along with many other people from Cape Verde, emigrated to different parts of the world.

Almost two-thirds of the 1 million Cape Verdians alive today live abroad. Most of Evora's siblings emigrated, but Evora chose to stay and continue singing.

Thirty years later, in the 1980s, a young Frenchman, captivated by her singing, convinced her to go with him to Paris to record. In 1988 she released her first album, but it was her album released in 1992, *Miss Perfumado,* that made her an international star. She was then a fifty-two-year-old grandmother. Her self-titled 1995 album was called "Best of the Year" and nominated for a Grammy. She has become known as the "Barefoot Diva" because she chooses to appear on stage in her bare feet in support of the disadvantaged women and children of her country. Her songs speak of her country's history of isolation, of the slave trade, and of emigration. Although her voice would lend itself well to jazz, Evora sings only morna.

DiNAH WASHiNGTON
Queen of the Blues

DINAH WASHINGTON was a much-married, hard-living woman with a heart of gold and a voice that was equally mesmerizing singing blues or pop. The future "Queen of the Blues" was born Ruth Lee Jones in Tuscaloosa, Alabama, to a poor but musically talented family. In 1928 the family moved to Chicago. In addition to doing domestic work, her mother earned money by playing piano at church. She taught her daughter to play piano at a young age, and Ruth was soon playing and singing in church, gaining such popularity that her mother formed a singing group around her and toured Black churches around the country. They made very little money with this venture, however, and the family continued to struggle in poverty.

In her teens, Ruth began listening to secular music and singing popular songs. Her mother was not pleased. Ruth won an amateur contest at the age of fifteen and began to perform at local nightclubs under an assumed name so that her mother wouldn't know.

In 1940 she joined the Sallie Martin Colored Ladies Quartet and stayed with them for three years. Still unable to make enough money, she returned to Chicago to perform in nightclubs. She met and married John Young, who became her agent and the first of her seven husbands.

Dinah Washington

In 1942 the manager of the Garrick Lounge in Chicago changed Ruth's name to Dinah Washington for billing and promotional reasons. That year she began touring with Lionel Hampton's orchestra, but left his group in 1945 because of differences she had with him about money. The legend is that she had to pull a gun on Hampton to get him to let her out of her contract.

She made her first solo recording in December 1945 and signed an exclusive recording contract with Mercury Records in early 1946. She spent sixteen years at Mercury and had forty-five songs on Billboard's Rhythm and Blues charts during that time. She

MARIE DAULNE: MUSICAL MELTING POT

This chanteuse comes by her multiculturalism naturally. Marie Daulne was born in the Democratic Republic of Congo (then Zaire) in 1964 to a Belgian father and a Zairian mother at a time of political upheaval in her country. After her father was killed during a period of "ethnic cleansing," her mother escaped with her children into the forest; eventually a government military patrol helped them escape the country and travel to Belgium, where her father's family welcomed them. Marie was raised as a Belgian child, her African heritage suppressed. While she was recuperating from a broken leg in 1986, this gifted athlete began to re-evaluate her ambition to participate in the Olympic games and also began listening to pygmy songs. Feeling the time was right to explore her heritage, she visited her mother's village in Zaire for the first time; when she returned to Belgium, she formed the first incarnation of Zap Mama, an a cappella women's group—*zap* for zapping from culture to culture, and *mama* for Mother Earth. Her eclectic background is reflected in her music, combining African, Arabic, reggae, soul, and gospel influences. A Zap Mama concert is a musical trip around the world. For Marie there is one culture, one that incorporates all nationalities and customs.

recorded with leading musicians of the time, such as Count Basie, Dizzy Gillespie, and Mitch Miller.

She was known both for her hair-trigger temper and her generosity. She often gave her friends expensive gifts and gave free concerts in Black communities. She also gave financial support to Martin Luther King, Jr., and generously supported the careers of many up-and-coming young stars, among them Redd Foxx, Johnny Mathis, Leslie Uggams, and Quincy Jones.

Although she had earned the title "Queen of the Blues," she also recorded many pop songs. Nonetheless, Mercury continued to promote her as a rhythm and blues vocalist, and, unhappy with this limitation on her career, she left Mercury in 1961 and signed with Roulette Records. Shortly afterward, her career went into a decline, along with her finances. The years of touring, the diet pills and sleeping pills, along with the heavy drinking, began to take their toll on her health. She died just before Christmas 1963 at the age of thirty-nine from an accidental overdose of sleeping pills combined with alcohol.

EARTHA KiTT

From Cotton to Caviar

EARTHA KITT has been one of the sexiest women entertainers in the world for nearly six decades. The talented songstress and actress was born to sharecroppers in South Carolina in 1928. Abandoned by their parents, Eartha and her sister were raised in a foster family until 1936, when they were sent to live with an aunt in New York.

In the Puerto Rican-Italian section of New York in which they lived, Eartha developed an ear for languages (she is fluent in six) and a love of song and dance. She attended the New York School of the Performing Arts, where she won prizes in dramatics, partly due to her unique voice. She was also adept at baseball and track and field, and was a champion pole vaulter.

She left school at fourteen to work in a sweatshop, sewing uniforms for the Army and managing to save some of her money for piano lessons. At the age of sixteen a friend introduced her to Katherine Dunham, at the time one of the most well-known Black dancers in the world. Dunham helped Kitt get a dance scholarship. She premiered with the Dunham Dance Group in May 1945 and toured the United States, Mexico, South America, and Europe as a featured soloist, even appearing before the royal family in London.

When the troupe returned to the United States in 1948, Kitt remained behind in Paris, singing at a popular nightclub and taking Paris by storm, and traveling to many European cities as well as to the Mediterranean and Egypt. Her gowns and facility with languages won almost as much praise as her singing.

Orson Welles offered her the role of Helen of Troy in his stage production of *Faust*. Her first legitimate stage role brought her more rave reviews. In 1952 her engagement at the Blue Angel nightclub in New York City broke the

The most exciting men in my life have been the men who have never taken me to bed. One can lose a great friend by going to bed with them.

—Eartha Kitt

159

all-time attendance record. She recorded *The Eartha Kitt Album* and appeared in *New Faces,* a film version of a live revue she had appeared in earlier. Her recording of "Santa Baby," made in 1953, is still a seasonal favorite and was followed by appearances on television shows such as *Toast of the Town, The Colgate Comedy Hour,* and Edward R. Murrow's *Person to Person.* She took a break in 1956 to write her autobiography, then returned to Broadway to play in Shinbone Alley in 1957. Later, she took on film roles in *St. Louis Blues* and *Anna Lucasta.*

She married in 1960, had a daughter in 1962, and was divorced in 1965. In the meanwhile she was awarded the Golden Rose of Montreux for a Swedish television production in 1962. In 1965–1966, she toured as Doris W in the stage production of *The Owl and the Pussycat.* She was now an established international star. Perhaps her most widely known role was as the sexy Catwoman on the *Batman* television series in 1967.

An incident in 1968 changed her life. She was invited to a White House function hosted by Lady Bird Johnson and used the occasion to speak out against racial and social problems in the United States and against the United States' involvement in the

ELIZABETH TAYLOR GREENFIELD: THE BLACK SWAN

Elizabeth Taylor Greenfield earned the sobriquet "The Black Swan" because of the sweetness and range of her voice. Born in Natchez, Mississippi, in 1819, she became the best-known Black concert artist of her day, touring the United States and Canada. She appeared before Queen Victoria on May 10, 1853, making her the first Black singer to give a command performance for royalty.

Vietnam War. Overnight she became a hero to the antiwar and civil rights movements, and an outcast among conservative politicians. She was ridiculed in the press, investigated by the CIA and the FBI, and allegedly blacklisted. Although she was awarded the Woman of the Year award by the National Association of Negro Musicians that year, her career came to a near standstill.

Since then, she has worked primarily in Europe as a cabaret singer. In 1978, she made a brief appearance on Broadway and returned to the White House as a guest of President Jimmy Carter. She experienced a public revival in the United States with her appearance at Carnegie Hall in 1985 and scored a scene-stealing turn in Eddie Murphy's 1992 movie *Boomerang*. In 2000 she was nominated for a Tony award for her role on Broadway in *The Wild Party*. She continues to enjoy a cabaret career at age seventy-two.

Kitt has expressed no resentment about the ups and downs she has experienced in her career. "Overall," she notes, "I've had a very good life, a life of cotton and caviar. . . ."

SiPPiE WALLACE
The Texas Nightingale

BORN BEULAH WALLACE on November 1, 1898, in Houston, Texas, she was nicknamed Sippie by her siblings. She grew up singing in the family church. Her parents were very religious people who did not approve of the blues music for which Sippie would become famous. Her brother George moved to New Orleans in 1912 in pursuit of a musical career, and Sippie soon followed. Among the friends of her brother that she met while she was there were the famous trumpeter, King Oliver, and his protégé, Louis Armstrong.

In 1918, after both of her parents had died, she went home to Houston to take care of her younger siblings. Shortly thereafter, her career as a singer really began when she took a job as maid and stage assistant to a snakedancer. They toured Texas, and Sippie's singing earned her the name "Texas Nightingale." Soon she was making enough money as a singer to give up her job as a maid.

Sippie Wallace

Brother George sent for her to come to his new home in Chicago, where he had made a name for himself as a composer and music publisher. She brought their brother Hersal along and the three formed a trio. Through George's connections they became famous recording artists.

Soon Sippie was a solo act, a regular headliner on the Theater Owners Booking Association circuit. But her personal life was filled with sorrow. Both of her marriages ended in divorce. Her oldest sister died in 1925, her brother Hersal died in 1926 at the age of sixteen from food poisoning, and in 1928 George was killed by a streetcar on the streets of Chicago. As if that weren't enough, her career took a downturn during the Great Depression. Her stage bookings petered out and by 1932 she had faded into obscurity. Church and family became the focus of her life for the next three decades. In the 1960s, a friend convinced her to come out of retirement to work the folk-blues festival circuit that had sprung up across the country.

She went to Europe in 1966 and thrilled a new generation with her gutsy, honky-tonk style. The Storyville label recorded her Copenhagen performance; reviewers compared her to Bessie Smith. In 1977, at age eighty, she performed at Lincoln Center's Avery Fisher Hall. She was still performing, despite age and arthritis, six months before her death in 1986.

PEARL PRIMUS
▲▲▲▲▲▲▲▲▲▲▲▲▲▲▲▲▲▲▲▲▲▲▲▲▲

Renaissance Woman

IF NOT FOR the ineptitude of the government, and perhaps a bit of racial prejudice, Pearl Primus would probably have become a fine doctor. Instead she was an outstanding anthropologist, choreographer, dancer, teacher, storyteller, and lecturer on African dance and African American studies.

Pearl was born in 1919 on the island of Trinidad in the Caribbean. When she was young her family, like many families before them, moved to the United States looking for a better life. She graduated from Hunter College in New York City in 1940 with a degree in biology and pre-med sciences, and planned to become a doctor. Her race kept her from finding a laboratory job, so she enrolled in the National Youth Administration (NYA), which existed from 1935 to 1945 as part of the Works Progress Administration (WPA) established during the Great Depression. The NYA provided work training and part-time employment for unemployed young people and needy students. Rather than being given an assignment in her field, she was sent to a dance group.

She took effortlessly to dancing, winning a scholarship with the New Dance Group. She became a teacher with the group and premiered her first choreographed work in 1943. But she still entertained notions of becoming a doctor. The matter was brought to a head when she was offered a dancing engagement at the Café Society Downtown. She stood at a crossroad—should she go back to

OTHER BLUES FIRSTS

- Mamie Smith became the first Black woman to make a record when she recorded "You Can't Keep a Good Man Down" in 1920. She also recorded the first blues song, "Crazy Blues," which sold 790,000 copies its first year.

- "Downhearted Blues/Gulf Coast Blues," recorded in 1923 by Bessie Smith, was the first million-selling record by a Black person.
- Ma (Gertrude) Rainey was the first professional blues singer.

school to complete her education as a doctor or continue with the dancing she had come to love?

She finally decided to accept the dance offer and performed at the nightclub for almost a year, where she was a hit. In 1948 she was awarded a Rosenwald Foundation Fellowship, which allowed her to spend eighteen months traveling through Africa, studying dance. She often claimed that she had learned the dances of Africa from her grandfather in her dreams. It was the authenticity of her "dreamed" steps that led the foundation to offer her the grant. In later years she returned to Africa several times, and was the director of Liberia's Performing Arts Center for two years.

Primus was studying Caribbean dance forms in the West Indies when she met Percival Borde. They opened a dance school in New York City where they both taught dance and anthropology. In 1955 they solidified the partnership by marrying. They taught and danced all over the United States and toured Africa with their dance troupe. Primus expressed her ideas about social conditions through her dance, combining African, African American, and Caribbean influences. Some of her dances have become classics, such as *Strange Fruit,* a choreographed commentary on lynching.

In 1978, Primus received her Ph.D. in anthropology from New York University. She lectured throughout the world and was professor of ethnic studies at Amherst College in Massachusetts and director of the Pearl Primus Dance Language Institute. After her

> Dance is my medicine. It's the scream which eases for a while the terrible frustration common to all human beings who, because of race, creed, or color are "invisible."
>
> **—Pearl Primus**

165

Pearl Primus was one of many Black artists who benefited from a Rosenwald Award. Julius Rosenwald founded the fund in 1917 with a threefold goal: to improve rural education, especially in the South; to develop leadership among Black and white Southerners through fellowships; and to facilitate advanced education and health among African Americans. Rosenwald had started out manufacturing suits, then partnered with Richard Sears after Alvah Roebuck retired from running Sears, Roebuck. He eventually became chairman of the board of the company after Sears' resignation in 1908, and held the position until he died in 1932. His position in the company assured, he began a second career as a philanthropist. In 1911 he met with Booker T. Washington and agreed to raise $50,000 for Washington's Tuskegee Institute. He also agreed to support the building of schools and YMCAs for Blacks, agreeing to contribute $25,000 if other parties could raise $75,000. When Rosenwald died he had contributed $4.4 million to build 5,357 schools in the South; these funds were matched by $4.7 million from African Americans. No school was built unless Blacks were also willing to contribute. Rosenwald believed in using philanthropy to inspire self-sufficiency. In 1917 he created the Rosenwald Fund, gradually turning 180,000 shares of Sears, Roebuck stock over to the fund. In 1927 he increased the fund's endowment to $20 million by adding another 20,000 shares, but he insisted that the Julius Rosenwald Fund spend itself out of existence twenty-five years after his death. He did not believe in perpetual endowments. "By adopting a policy of using the Fund within this generation, we may avoid those tendencies toward bureaucracy and a formal or perfunctory attitude toward the work which almost inevitably develop in organizations which prolong their existence indefinitely. Coming generations can be relied upon to provide for their own needs as they arise." The trustees were so good at following Rosenwald's instructions that they were out of money in 1948, a full decade before they were required to cease to exist.

husband died in 1979, she stopped performing to take up the position of director of the Cora P. Maloney College, a Black Studies school at the State University of New York in Buffalo. She was the first recipient of the Balasaraswati/Joy Ann Dewey Beinecke Chair for Distinguished Teaching and was awarded the National Medal of the Arts by the President of the United States in 1991 in recognition of her contribution to the exploration of socially significant themes through dance. Other awards bestowed upon her before her death were the Distinguished Service Award from the Association of American Anthropologists, an honorary doctorate from Spelman College, and the Star of Africa from the Liberian government. She died in 1994.

JUDiTH JAMiSON
Creating a Life Through Dance

HER FATHER WAS a steelworker and part-time pianist and singer, and he taught Judith to play the piano. When she was six, her parents enrolled her in dance classes. She would rather dance than be on the playground. After she finished high school, Judith enrolled at Fisk University in Nashville, Tennessee, as a psychology major. She transferred to the Philadelphia Dance Academy (now the University of the Arts) when she decided to pursue a career in dance.

In 1964, Agnes de Mille, who was teaching a master class at Judith's school, invited her to dance in the premiere of de Mille's ballet, *The Four Marys*, at Lincoln Center in New York. After the ballet closed, Judith could not find another dancing job and, needing money, took one operating the Log-Flume Ride at the 1964 World's Fair. She was not there for long. In 1965 she debuted with the Alvin Ailey Dance Company (now the Alvin Ailey American Dance Theater), the most successful racially integrated dance company in the United States. In a short time she was Ailey's leading dancer. She became a star in 1971, performing one of the longest (fifteen minutes) and most demanding solos in dance. The piece, called *Cry*, was created especially for her by Ailey. It became her signature piece. The company toured the United States, Russia, France, India, Cuba, Sweden, and Japan. She also appeared as a guest artist with other companies both in the United States and Europe.

> We can go on talking about racism and who treated whom badly, but what are you going to do about it? Are you going to wallow in that or are you going to create your own agenda?
>
> —**Judith Jamison**

President Nixon appointed her an advisor to the National Council on the Arts in 1972. In 1976 she danced with Mikhail Baryshnikov in a program presented by the Ailey Company to honor Duke Ellington. In 1980 she starred in the Broadway production, *Sophisticated Ladies*. Her first work of choreography, *Divining*, premiered in 1984. In 1989, Alvin Ailey died and Judith Jamison became the director and choreographer of the company and the director of its school, which has more than 3,000 students. She continues in that position today.

DiANA SANDS
▲▲▲▲▲▲▲▲▲▲▲▲▲▲▲▲▲▲▲▲▲▲▲

Destined for the Silver Screen

DIANA SANDS was one of the leading Black stage actresses in the late 1950s. She was the youngest of three children raised in the Bronx, New York. Unlike many other aspiring actors, her parents were supportive of her career choice. As a child, Diana attended elementary school in Elmsford, New York. There were few other Black people there, and the family returned to Manhattan because of racial discrimination. There Diana attended the High School of the Performing Arts and began her acting career. After graduation she "paid her dues," touring as a carnival singer, taking $15-a-week acting jobs, doing show tours, living on various night jobs while taking daytime classes, living in furnished flats, and truly being a starving artist.

Diana began to make her mark in 1957, when she landed a role in *Land Beyond the River.* Following that she had singing roles in *The Egg and I* and *Another Evening with Harry Stoones.* But she almost missed the role that made her a star. By 1959 she had despaired of making it as an actress, and when the casting call went out for *Raisin in the Sun,* she didn't even want to audition. But she did, going on to win both the Outer Critics' Circle Award for best supporting actress and the *Variety* Critic's Award for the most promising young actress for her role as Beneatha Younger. She repeated the role in the film version and won the 1961 International Artists' Award for that performance.

1964 was an even better year. She won an Obie for *Living Premise* and a Tony nomination for her role in *Blues for Mr. Charlie.* And she married Lucien Happersberg, a Swiss artist, although they were divorced a few years later. Then she was cast opposite Alan Alda in *The Owl and the Pussycat.* The part was not written for a Black actress, but nothing in the play was changed to explain her race. Despite opposition and controversy, her performance was sensational, and she was again nominated for a Tony award. The London production in 1965 was equally acclaimed.

Diana also appeared in many television shows, garnering two Emmy nominations for her work on the small screen. She toured in leading roles in *Caesar and Cleopatra, Antony and Cleopatra,* and *Phaedra.* In 1968 she gave what many considered her finest performance, as the lead in George Bernard Shaw's *St. Joan.*

OTHER ACTING FIRSTS

- Madame Sul-Te-Wan became the first Black American to be hired by a major movie producer on a continuing basis when she was signed on by D. W. Griffith after he had seen her in *Birth of a Nation.*
- Hattie McDaniel was a singer and a vaudeville performer, but she is best known for her acting, having been the first Black person to win an Oscar for her supporting role as Mammy in *Gone with the Wind.*
- Sultry Dorothy Dandridge was the first Black nominated for an Oscar in a leading role for her portrayal of Carmen in *Carmen Jones,* a retelling of the classic opera tale with an all-Black cast. She broke another barrier with her role in *Island in the Sun,* in which she was cast opposite a white actor in the first silver screen exploration of interracial love.
- Diahann Carroll was the first Black woman to have her own television series, starring in *Julia* in 1968.

Good roles became harder for her to find in the 1970s. In 1973 she was planning to remarry and had been cast to star opposite James Earl Jones in the film *Claudine* when she was suddenly taken ill and Diahann Carrol had to take the role. Diana was hospitalized and died on September 21, 1973, of an inoperable tumor caused by lung cancer.

VALAiDA SNOW
▲▲▲▲▲▲▲▲▲▲▲▲▲▲▲▲▲▲▲▲

Queen of the Trumpet

VALAIDA SNOW was such a fine trumpeter that her nickname was Little Louis, a reference to Louis "Satchmo" Armstrong. She was born in 1900 into a musical family. Her mother taught her bass violin, cello, guitar, and other stringed instruments. Later she added dancing, singing, and composing to her repertoire. But she became best known for her talent on the trumpet.

She started out playing in small clubs in Pennsylvania and New Jersey. In 1922 she debuted at Harlem's Exclusive Club and moved on to Broadway in 1924's *Chocolate Dandies.* She appeared on stage in *Rhapsody in Black* that year and in *Blackbirds* in 1934. She also had parts in a few American and French films in the 1930s. She toured from the 1930s through the 1950s with the likes of Count Basie, Earl "Fatha" Hines, and Fletcher Henderson, cutting about forty records during that time.

Not only was she outstanding as a trumpeter, she liked to live large as well. Singer and pianist Bobby Short, who as a young man became infatuated with her, remembered her traveling "in an orchid-colored Mercedes-Benz, dressed in an orchid suit, her pet monkey rigged out in an orchid jacket and cap, with a chauffeur in orchid as well."

As was the case with many other African American artists, Valaida was more famous in Europe than in the United States. But Europe was also the site of her downfall. There is some mystery about what happened. She was arrested in Nazi-held Denmark, possibly accused of drug possession or theft. Whatever the reason, she was definitely in the wrong place at the wrong time: she was a non-Aryan in a Europe under Hitler's domination. She was sent to the Wester-Faengler concentration camp, where she was held for two years. She was freed in a prisoner swap and returned to the United States in 1941. When she got home, she weighed 70 pounds.

She was never the same again, although she did eventually return to performing. She played and recorded until her death of a cerebral hemorrhage backstage at a performance in New York in 1956. She never made public what had happened to her in the concentration camp.

YELENA KHANGA

▲▲▲▲▲▲▲▲▲▲▲▲▲▲▲▲▲▲▲▲▲▲▲▲▲▲▲▲▲▲▲

Black Russian

YELENA KHANGA is an international woman in several senses. She has an international career and also carries a mixture of the heritages of America, Russia, and Africa.

In 1928, Bertha Bialek, the daughter of a Polish-born rabbi, met Oliver Golden, the son of a slave from the Mississippi Delta, in a New York prison. They were both members of the American Communist Party and had been arrested at a union demonstration. They fell in love and married, which prompted Bertha's family to disown her. The couple tried living in Harlem, but they were not accepted there either, so they moved to Greenwich Village.

In 1931, Oliver was among sixteen African American agronomists hired by the Soviet Union to help develop a cotton industry in Uzbekistan, and he moved there with his wife. While there, Bertha taught English at the local university. When the other Americans returned to the United States, the Goldens chose to stay. They had a daughter, Lily, who eventually graduated from Moscow State University with a Ph.D. in history. Her specialty was African music and culture. She married Oxford-educated Abdullah Kassim Khanga, a diplomat-in-training from Tanzania. After the marriage, he forced strict Muslim rules of conduct on her. She was forbidden to have any contact with men if he was not present. His desire for a son was such that when daughter Yelena was born, he refused to pick up his wife and new baby from the hospital.

Tanzania gained its independence in 1964, and Abdullah became vice president from 1964 until 1969. Yelena and her mother remained in Russia. Then, in a series of political intrigues, he was arrested. He was never tried, and though it is assumed he was assassinated, his body was never found. Rumors abound that he is still in hiding, waiting for the time to be right for a rebellion.

Despite this tragedy, Yelena's mother took good care of her. As a teenager she was a champion tennis player, and she graduated from Moscow State University as a journalism major. It was while studying journalism that she became seriously interested in Black American history. Her graduation thesis was on the African American press.

After graduation, in the midst of *perestroika,* Yelena was hired by the *Moscow News.* In 1988 she became the first Russian journalist to participate in an exchange program with the *Christian Science Monitor* in the United States. She discovered that what she had thought was a monolithic Black American community was much more complex. She also realized that getting rid of legal segregation was much easier than eliminating the prejudice that produced it.

The U.S. media loved her, and she was featured in many magazine and newspaper articles and appeared on major network television shows. She also participated in the first Washington summit between presidents Gorbachev and Reagan. She was given a one-year fellowship by the Rockefeller Foundation to research her family roots. Out of that research came a book, *Soul to Soul: A Black Russian Jewish Woman's Search for Her Roots.*

She has lived in New York ever since; her mother has joined her. She discovered relatives in both New York and Mississippi. In 1991 she made her first trip to Tanzania, meeting her paternal grandmother in a remote village. Her grandmother kindly offered to find her a husband, but the proposed bridegroom was a seventy-four-year old man who already had three wives. Although she was officially welcomed in Tanzania, she was subjected to constant surveillance, just in case it turned out she was interested in taking up where her father had left off, but she received clandestine messages of support.

Her life took another interesting twist after she returned to New York. A Russian television producer called her up with the old "I'm going to make you a star" routine. Thinking it was a practical joke, Yelena refused. But the producer flew to New York from Moscow and convinced her he was serious. Now she spends one week each month in Russia taping a television talk show, *About Talk*. Yelena uses her forum to explore questions of sex, race, culture, and morals, hoping to help her audience to see these issues in a new light. The first show in Russia to openly discuss sexual matters, it is immensely popular and also draws great criticism from ultra-nationalist politicians.

But that is only one week out of her month. She spends the rest of her time in New York, where she performs with a comedy group in Brighton Beach. As of this writing, she is scheduled to host an upcoming Russian-language television show to be filmed in Brighton Beach.

ARTiSTS WITH ATTITUdE

EDMONiA LEWIS

Wildfire

▲▲▲▲▲▲▲▲▲▲▲▲▲▲▲▲▲▲▲▲▲▲▲▲▲

EDMONIA LEWIS was the first successful Black sculptor. She was born to a free Black father and a Chippewa mother in 1843, although she often claimed a later birth date. The family lived in Albany, New York, but Edmonia's mother would often visit her tribe in upstate New York, taking Edmonia with her. Edmonia's tribal nickname was Wildfire. When Edmonia was orphaned at age five, she went to live with the Chippewas, where she remained until she was twelve, earning a living making and selling moccasins.

In 1856 her brother Sunrise returned from the gold fields in California and arranged for Edmonia to attend school near Albany. In 1859, he sent her to Oberlin College in Oberlin, Ohio, where she finished her high school course and entered the liberal arts program. There, in fulfillment of a lifelong ambition, she began drawing. In her fourth year at Oberlin, a tragedy occurred that ended her college career: she was accused of poisoning two of her classmates. Although she was acquitted at her trial, she left Oberlin for Boston, where she began sculpting. There she met William Lloyd Garrison, the abolitionist. He introduced her to Edward Brackett, a well-known sculptor, who gave her sculptures to copy and critiqued her work. Her most important work from this period was a bust of Colonel Robert Shaw, the white commander of the 54th Massachusetts Regiment whose story was told in the movie *Glory*.

Throughout the Civil War, Lewis supported herself with her sculpture. In 1865, barely twenty years old, she traveled to Europe to study sculpture and settled in Rome, where she made a living copying classical sculptures and selling them to American tourists and fulfilling commissions for small portrait busts. Much of her work was shipped to her patrons in Boston.

Although Lewis produced commercial sculptures to keep body and soul together, her passion revolved around the issues of slavery and racial oppression, which were expressed in her sculptures *The*

Oberlin College in Ohio holds a special place in Black educational history. The college and the nearby town attracted many Blacks and anti-slavery people and were a stop on the Underground Railroad. Students at the college actively aided runaways. In 1835, the board of trustees of Oberlin voted to admit students of color. It was the first college in the United States to make this a policy. This momentous event gave free Blacks unfettered access to higher education. From 1835 to 1865 Oberlin, dubbed "the abolitionist school," was the educational birthing ground of Black leaders in many fields: religion, medicine, journalism, and the arts, among others.

Freed Woman and Her Child and *Forever Free*. She also expressed her Native American heritage in several pieces. One of the highlights of her career was the showing of her work *The Death of Cleopatra* at the Centennial Exposition in Philadelphia in 1876.

Lewis reached the height of her popularity in the 1870s, when her studio became a frequent stop for Americans on their European tours. Europeans were equally enchanted with her.

AUGUSTA SAVAGE
Creating a World with Her Hands

AUGUSTA SAVAGE was born February 29, 1892, in Green Cove Springs, Florida. She was the seventh child of fourteen. Early on she began modeling figures out of the red clay that filled the soil around her. One of her favorite subjects was ducks. Her father, a housepainter and strict Baptist minister, called her tiny sculptures graven images and tried to beat her artistic tendencies out of her. But he didn't stop her; she just learned to hide her work from him.

In 1907, at the age of fifteen, Augusta married John T. Moore. They had one child, a daughter they named Irene. Moore died a few years later, and Augusta returned to her family with her child. She and her daughter remained close throughout her life.

In 1915 her family moved to West Palm Beach, where her father had been appointed minister at a local church. Clay was not readily available there, but she found a small pottery factory where she was able to beg small amounts. She fashioned a small statue of the Virgin Mary, which her father happened to see. He was so impressed that he began to support her work.

She had returned to high school, where in her senior year the school board appointed her to teach modeling for the modest salary of $1 per day. Her work attracted the attention of the county fair superintendent, who allowed her to exhibit her work at the fair. She was not only awarded a special prize of $25, but earned an additional $150 for her sculptures.

Augusta hoped to use the money to move to New York City to study. But the money had to be used to help her family, and by the time she arrived in New York, she only had $4.60 left. She was forced to find work away from her sculpting, so she took a job as an apartment caretaker. The county fair superintendent had given her a letter of introduction to sculptor Solon Borglum, but she could not afford his fees and he would not consider taking a non-paying student. He did, however, write her a letter of recommendation to the registrar of Cooper Union, a public school in New York with free tuition for those who were accepted. On the basis of his recommendation and a sample piece she had created overnight, she won immediate entry.

The Cooper Union school board was very impressed with Augusta's hard work, and they gave her a scholarship to pay her living expenses. She completed the four-year course in three years.

Meanwhile, others were beginning to take note of her talent. The librarian at the Harlem branch of the New York Public Library, Sadie Peterson (Delaney)—one of the now-famous Delaney sisters—convinced the friends of the library to commission

Savage to do a portrait of W. E. B. Du Bois. This portrait led to commissions for portraits of other prominent Black leaders from other patrons of the arts, including one of the most well-known leaders, Marcus Garvey, who sat for her at his Harlem apartment. She was becoming well known among the Black elite.

Augusta Savage

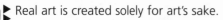

> Real art is created solely for art's sake.
>
> **—Augusta Savage**

In 1923 Augusta learned that the French government would host 100 female students at a summer sculpting school at Fontainbleau, outside Paris. She applied for and was granted one of the scholarships. Then she received a note that the scholarship had been withdrawn. At first the committee said it was a lack of references, but soon she learned that it was because she was Black.

Augusta was too angry to let this slight pass unnoticed. She protested loudly enough for the story be to front-page news in the New York press for days. Only one committee member, Hermon MacNeil, was brave enough to publicly admit his embarrassment. MacNeil asked Savage to work with him and she accepted. But the controversy earned her a reputation as a troublemaker. It is probable that she was excluded from many exhibits and galleries because of it.

More setbacks lay ahead. She married an official in Marcus Garvey's Black nationalist movement in 1923. He died five months later. In 1925, with the help of Du Bois, she received a scholarship to the Royal Academy of Fine Arts in Rome, Italy. She took a job as a laundress to earn money for her fare, but had to spend the money to help her aging parents and was forced to turn down the scholarship. In 1928 her brother died, and her entire family came to live with her in New York. Shortly afterward her father died. She gave up her dreams of studying abroad in order to take care of her family.

All was not lost. In 1929 the executive secretary of the National Urban League asked the Julius Rosenwald Fund to award Augusta a fellowship to study in Paris. After viewing her work, the committee raised their scholarship offer from $1,500 to $1,800. The Harlem community held parties to raise money for her living expenses.

The Rosenwald Fund was so pleased with her work abroad that in 1931 they awarded her a second scholarship. She also won a grant from the Carnegie Foundation that allowed her to travel through France, Germany, and Belgium, continuing her studies.

In 1932 she returned to New York and began making her living doing portrait sculpture. But this was the Great Depression, and money was scarce. She began teaching, using a $1,500 Carnegie Foundation grant to start the Savage Studio of Arts and Crafts. There she trained and influenced many young Black artists.

In 1933 she helped to organize the Vanguard Club, a salon that met weekly to discuss social and economic issues important to

MAY HOWARD JACKSON: AFROCENTRIC AESTHETIC

After attending public schools in Philadelphia, May Howard Jackson was enrolled in Todd's Art School. In 1895 Jackson's artistic talent earned her a scholarship to the Pennsylvania Academy of Fine Arts; it was the first scholarship to be awarded to a Black woman. Her work, centering on the realistic portrayal of Black people, was not well received in the art world, but this was not due to a lack of talent. The prevailing images of Black people at the time were stereotypes; realistic portrayals of Black people such as those created by May were not appreciated.

The lack of acceptance of her work made her bitter and angry, but she persevered and was instrumental in the establishment of an Afrocentric aesthetic. She did portrait busts of many Black leaders, among them Paul Laurence Dunbar and W. E. B. Du Bois. She staged several successful exhibitions and was awarded the Bronze Award from the Harmon Foundation's Achievements for Negroes in the Fine Arts. Unfortunately, many of her works have been lost. Some that remain are at Dunbar High School in Washington, D.C., and at Howard University.

Black artists. When it became a gathering place for Harlem's communist contingent, she withdrew from the group. She was also active in bringing Black artists to the attention of the Works Projects Administration (WPA), and she helped organize the Harlem Artists' Guild. In 1934 she became the first Black member of the National Association of Women Painters and Sculptors.

In 1937 she was appointed director of the Harlem Community Center, a WPA project. Her friends were afraid that she was being distracted from her own sculpting. She replied, "I have created nothing really beautiful, really lasting. But if I can inspire one of these youngsters to develop the talent I know they possess, then my monument will be in their work. No one could ask more than that."

Soon after her appointment, she became the only Black woman invited to produce a sculpture for the 1939 New York World's Fair. She could not afford to cast the resulting piece, *The Harp,* in bronze. The plaster original was bulldozed with the rest of the exhibits.

META FULLER

▲▲▲▲▲▲▲▲▲▲▲▲▲▲▲▲▲▲▲▲▲▲▲▲▲▲▲▲

Pan-African Artist

META FULLER was another artist who drew on African influences in her art. Born in Philadelphia in 1877, she was raised in a middle-class Black family. She attended both the Pennsylvania Museum and School for the Industrial Arts and the Pennsylvania Academy of the Fine Arts, followed by study with Auguste Rodin in Paris.

In 1914 she created her most famous sculpture, *Ethiopia Awakening,* a powerful piece symbolizing the emergence of the New Negro. The lower half of the piece is a partially wrapped mummy, while the upper half has the hair and shoulders of a beautiful Black woman wearing the headdress of an ancient Egyptian queen.

Through her work Fuller intended to awaken Black people to their majestic African heritage. Although she never lived in Harlem and was not part of the Harlem Renaissance, her art and sensibilities contributed to it. Other artists had used African art as inspiration before, but Fuller was the first to rely on it almost exclusively.

JACKiE ORMES
▲▲▲▲▲▲▲▲▲▲▲▲▲▲▲▲▲▲▲▲▲
Groundbreaking Cartoonist

IN THE LATE 1930s, Jackie Ormes made history by creating the nationally syndicated cartoon strips "Torchy Brown," "Patty Jo 'n' Ginger," and "Candy." Until the 1990s, she was the only Black woman cartoonist to be nationally syndicated.

Her father was an artist who passed his talent along to his daughter. She studied art in school and then went to work for the *Pittsburgh Courier* around 1936, beginning as a feature writer. Soon she began developing the "Torchy" strip, which was first published on May 1, 1937. Torchy was a farm girl from the South

Barbara Brandon is the first Black woman cartoonist to be nationally syndicated in white newspapers. Her strip, "Where I'm Coming From," was first published in the *Detroit Free Press* and was syndicated in 1991. She came by her talent naturally: her father, Brumsic Brandon, Jr., created the "Luther" comic strip in the late 1960s.

who moved to Harlem and became a newspaper reporter.

Jackie's given name was Zelda Jackson. After she married Earl Ormes, she created her pen name of Jackie Ormes by combining her family name and her married name. She moved to Chicago in the early 1940s to work for the *Chicago Defender* as a general assignment reporter and to attend classes at the Art Institute of Chicago. There she developed her second strip, "Patty Jo 'n' Ginger," about two sisters. The strip addressed many political issues, among them sex roles, segregation, and educational inequalities.

Her strips were syndicated nationally in Black newspapers, but she never broke into white media. She retired in the late 1960s due to rheumatoid arthritis, although she remained active in the Chicago community, serving on the board of directors of the Du Sable Museum of African-American History and Art.

ELiZABETH CATLETT
Public Artist

ELIZABETH CATLETT played an important role in the art world of the 1940s and '50s in both the United States and Mexico. Graduating from high school with honors in 1933, she took the entrance examinations for the Carnegie Institute of Technology in Pittsburgh but was rejected because of her race. Instead, she studied art at Howard University, where she was taught by some of the most influential figures in African American art at the time. At Howard, she was exposed to African as well as Western art. On the advice of one of her teachers, she began working with the Federal Art Project of the Works Progress Administration (WPA). While researching techniques for a mural she wanted to paint, she was introduced to the Mexican muralists who were to become a huge influence on her work.

She earned her B.S. in art from Howard in 1937 at the age of eighteen, graduating cum laude, then taught high school art and supervised art programs for eight elementary schools in Durham, North Carolina. She went on to graduate

> I want to do large, public works. I want public art to have meaning for Black people so they will have some art they can identify with.
>
> **—Elizabeth Catlett**

school at the University of Iowa, where she studied with Grant Wood, completing her master's degree in art in 1940 and becoming the first person to earn a master's degree in sculpture at the school. Her thesis piece won the first place award in sculpture in the American Negro Exposition in Chicago the following year.

During this time, she met and married Charles White, a painter and printmaker, and they moved to New Orleans, where Elizabeth was head of the art department at Dillard University. They later moved to New York City, where she continued to study and perfect her techniques. In 1945 she was awarded a Julius Rosenwald Fellowship (see sidebar on page 166). Together Elizabeth and Charles went to Mexico in 1946 to work with the Taller de Grafica Popular (TGP), a collective of socially involved printmakers. Although Elizabeth and Charles divorced, she continued to work with the TGP.

Her work, while providing a strong voice for Black women and other women of color, also exhibited Elizabeth's empathy with humanity, her feminist leanings, and her opposition to oppression of all women. She combined modernist, social realist, expressionist, African, and pre-Hispanic styles to express her ideas. Over time her style moved from realism to more abstract representations.

She married Mexican painter Francisco Mora in 1947; they had three sons. Both she and Francisco worked with the TGP until 1966. In 1958 she became a professor of sculpture in the National School of Fine Arts at the Universidad Nacional Autonoma de Mexico, becoming in 1959 the head of the sculpture department, a position she held until she retired in 1976.

Because Elizabeth had been politically active in Mexico, she was named an "undesirable" during the McCarthy era in the United States. She could no longer travel to the United States, and she became a Mexican citizen. In 1974, after a campaign by many young Black American artists, politicians, museum directors, and religious leaders, her undesirable status was lifted.

Elizabeth sculpts in many media, including marble, limestone, bronze, terracotta, and wood. She also does printmaking. Her subjects are Black and Mexican, primarily women. Through her work she seeks to express maternity, love, feminine beauty, and female leadership, among other qualities. Her works are in public spaces in both the United States and Mexico, including the Metropolitan

Museum of Art in New York City and the National Politechnical Institute in Mexico, and are shown in major museums internationally. Just as important to her is that her works are shown at churches or social clubs, where they are accessible to all people.

PHiLiPPA SCHUYLER
Piano Prodigy

PHILIPPA SCHUYLER was raised in a family with a deep and abiding interest in intellectual matters and the arts. Her father was a well-known Black writer. Her mother was the daughter of a wealthy white Texas ranching and banking family.

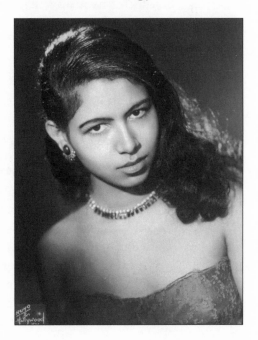

She was a prodigy from the beginning; she walked at eight months, was reading at two years, and played the piano at three. A year later she was performing her own piano compositions on the radio. At seven she was on tour, completing her first orchestral work at thirteen. She graduated from high school at fifteen, after which she continued to tour, visiting more than eighty countries and giving command performances for Ethiopia's Haile Selassie and Queen Elizabeth of Belgium.

Shortly after her high school graduation she wrote *The Rhapsody of Youth* to celebrate the inauguration of Haitian president Paul Magloire, for which she received the Haitian Decoration of Honor and Merit. During her life she wrote five books. She was also fluent in several languages and was a respected lecturer.

To further her writing career, she started working as a news correspondent. Her last assignment was to Vietnam in 1967. While helping to remove Catholic schoolchildren from Hue to Da Nang, which was relatively safe at the time, her helicopter crashed and she was killed.

NORMA SKLAREK

Pioneering Architect

NORMA SKLAREK has created a fistful of firsts in the field of architecture. She was born in New York City in 1928 and graduated from Columbia University's Barnard College with a degree in architecture in 1950.

She then became the first female African American licensed architect in the United States, gaining her New York license in 1954 and her California one in 1962. At the Los Angeles-based company Gruen and Associates, she became the first African American woman to be a director of architecture and in 1966 became the first woman Fellow of the American Institute of Architects.

In 1985 she became the first African American woman to form her own architectural firm, which is one of the largest totally woman-owned architectural firms in the United States. She held the distinction of being the only African American woman architect until the 1980s.

Among her designing credits are San Francisco's Fox Plaza, Terminal One at Los Angeles International Airport, San Bernardino's City Hall, and the U.S. Embassy in Tokyo.

> Architecture should be working on improving the environment of people in their homes, in their places of work, and their places of recreation. It should be functional and pleasant, not just in the image of the ego of the architect.
>
> **—Norma Sklarek**

FAITH RiNGGOLD
Artist Storyteller

FAITH RINGGOLD uses many artistic styles and media to express herself. She is a world-renowned painter, sculptor, and performance artist.

Growing up in New York City in the 1930s, she realized early on that she wanted to be an artist. As a child she suffered from asthma, which forced her to spend a lot of time at home with her mother, a fashion designer. Her mother taught her to sew and also took her to museums and shows. She attended City College in New York, earning both a B.A. and M.A. in art. In school she was trained in the classical Western traditions of art. Her attempts to paint Black people were thwarted. Discouraged, she went to Europe after graduation and began painting in the French Impressionist style. When she returned to New York with her still lifes, she was told that a Black woman could not paint European art. She was caught in the traditional paradox facing Black artists: she was told she could not paint in the European style but was not given any other training.

In 1963 she began to train herself, studying African art while reading James Baldwin and Amiri Baraka. Her thinking and work were greatly influenced by the Black political movement occurring at the time. Her work from that time reflects African influences in its use of matte tones and interlocking geometric shapes. In the early 1970s, her work began to focus on Black women and the need for them to speak out.

▶ HARRIET POWERS: TELLING STORIES IN CLOTH

Harriet Powers was a quiltmaker extraordinaire, but only two of her quilts remain. She was born into slavery in 1837 and after emancipation settled down to the life of a homemaker in Clarke County, Georgia, with her farmer husband. In 1886 she made a story quilt that depicted tales from the Bible by appliquéing almost 300 scraps of cloth. She sold this masterpiece for $5 to a young white teacher named Jennie Smith, supplying Smith with captions for each picture in the quilt. It now belongs to the Smithsonian Institution's National Museum of American History. She worked on her second story quilt, called "The Creation of the Animals," from 1895 until 1898. This is another work depicting Bible stories, along with folklore, and it now hangs in the Museum of Fine Arts in Boston. We can only wonder what other of her artistic endeavors have been lost over time.

Both Black male artists and the white art world were critical of Ringgold's work. Whites thought her work too political, while Black men thought it too Africanized and criticized her use of soft, female media. She was not alone. Black artists were ignored in exhibits and retrospectives organized by whites, and Black women were often excluded from exhibitions put together by Black men. Ringgold joined the Ad Hoc Committee on Women Artists and Students for Black Liberation, and in 1971 she and two other women artists put together a show of Black women artists called "Where We At."

In the mid-1970s, Ringgold added performance art to her repertoire, using her masks and soft sculptures. After her mother's death in 1981, Ringgold began making quilts in her honor. These memorial quilts evolved into her famous story quilts, which incorporate both painting and quilting. In 1992 she won the Caldecott Honor Book Award and the Coretta Scott King Illustrator Award for her children's book, *Tar Beach*.

Over the years, Ringgold has won many awards, including the National Endowment for the Arts Awards for sculpture, the New York Foundation for the Arts Award for painting, and the Creative Artists Public Service Award. She now splits her time between San Diego, where she is a professor of fine art, and her New York City art studio.

WONDERFUL
WORD
SMITHS

LUCY TERRY PRiNCE

Poetic Historian

BORN IN AFRICA in 1730, Lucy Terry Prince was kidnapped as a baby. At the age of five, she was sold in Rhode Island to Ensign Ebeneezer Wells, who lived in Deerfield, Massachusetts, located on the northernmost edge of the colony and adjacent to Indian territory. Not much is known about her life until she was sixteen, when she wrote a poem entitled "The Bars Fight." *Bar* was a colonial word for meadow, and the poem was based on a massacre of two colonial families by sixty Indians in an area outside Deerfield. This is believed to be the first poem written by an American slave, and it is still considered to be the best description of the raid on record. Lucy became somewhat of a local celebrity. The original of the poem has been lost, but it was passed down orally until it was printed for the first time in 1855.

She married Abijah Prince, who was twenty-four years her senior and a former slave who had gained his freedom after serving in the French and Indian War. He owned a large farm in Sunderland, Vermont, where he was one of the original town founders.

They moved to Guilford, Vermont, in 1760 after Abijah inherited 100 acres there. Although they were threatened by their white neighbors, they stayed on. They had six children whom Lucy wanted to attend college. She protested the discrimination against Blacks in education, speaking for three hours before the governor's council, but she was unsuccessful. She gained a national reputation for her speaking ability, eventually speaking before the Supreme Court in a case against a land-grabbing neighbor. Presiding Justice Samuel Chase is reported to have said that Lucy's oratory was superior to that of any Vermont lawyer in the court.

PHILLiS WHEATLEY

Pioneering Poetess

AS THE AUTHOR of a volume of poetry titled *Poems on Various Subjects, Religious and Moral,* which was published in 1773, Phillis Wheatley was the first Black person ever published in the United States and was quite famous in her day for her brilliance.

Most present-day scholars agree that she was probably born to the Fulani tribe in Gambia in West Africa. She was about seven when she was kidnapped and shipped to Boston, where she was sold into slavery in 1761. Named Phillis after the ship that had brought her to America, she was purchased by the Wheatley family, who taught her to read the English Bible. She mastered reading and writing in English in sixteen months and then began to learn Latin. According to her master, she also knew some astronomy, geography, and ancient history, and was familiar with the Latin classics. In 1767, at the age of fourteen, she wrote her first poem. The Wheatleys encouraged her writing, providing her with paper and pen.

In December 1767, the *Newport Mercury* printed her first published poem. It gained her some fame and she began to be received in literary and social circles that normally would have been forbidden to her. Although she could mingle with white people, she was not allowed to dine with them because she was a slave. In 1772 she began to consider publishing a volume of her poetry, but the racial atmosphere in Boston would not tolerate such a thing. John Wheatley made inquiries in England for her and found her a patron in the Countess of Huntington, who, after confirming that the poems were indeed written by an African girl, provided financial backing for their publication. Wheatley dedicated the book to the Countess when it was published in 1773.

Phyllis Wheatly

Wheatley had always had a frail con-
stitution, and her health began to
weaken further. The Wheatleys thought
a trip abroad might be good for her and
sent her to London, where the Countess
provided her an entree into society and
she became a cause celebré. Everyone in
high society wanted a peek at this brainy
young slave.

After Wheatley's return to Boston, Mrs. Wheatley died. In 1778,
John Wheatley passed away, and Phillis was freed. That same year
she married a Boston grocer. Unfortunately, her husband's profli-
gate ways led them into poverty. Wheatley worked in a boarding
house to help support herself and her family. She died on December 5, 1784, at the age of thirty-one, and the death of her one sur-
viving child followed closely afterward. They were buried
together, although the location of the grave is unknown. She had
written another manuscript, some 300 pages of poetry, which was
never published and has never been recovered.

NELLA LARSEN

Controversial Novelist

NELLA LARSEN was one of the first writers bold enough to write
about Black female sexuality. Born in Chicago, her mother was

Danish and her father was a Black man from the Danish Virgin Islands. Shortly after her birth in 1891, her parents separated. Her mother remarried a white man named Larsen, and Nella took his last name.

After graduating from Chicago's public schools, she attended Fisk University's Normal School, then spent two years at the University of Copenhagen. In 1912 she went to New York and trained as a nurse. After graduation she worked as the head nurse at John Andrew Memorial Hospital and Nurse Training School, which was affiliated with Tuskegee Institute in Alabama. In 1916 she returned to New York City and continued to work as a nurse.

Not long after, she met and married Elmer Imes, a physicist, and began to meet people involved in the growing arts movement in Harlem, a movement that became known as the Harlem Renaissance. Her interest in literature surfaced in this environment. In 1921 she quit her nursing job to take up a post at the New York Public Library's 135th Street branch in Harlem, while also attending library school at Columbia University. She worked at the library until 1926, honing her writing skills, publishing several short fiction pieces, and working on her first novel, *Quicksand*, which received critical acclaim after its publication in 1928.

As the product of a mixed marriage, Nella longed to be accepted in both Black and white worlds. The

> Helga Crane meant . . . to have a home . . . in Harlem. . . . Everything was there, vice and goodness, sadness and gaiety, ignorance and wisdom, ugliness and beauty, poverty and richness. And it seemed to her that somehow of goodness, gaiety, wisdom, and beauty always there was a little more than of vice, sadness, ignorance, and ugliness. It was only riches that did not quite transcend poverty.
>
> **—From *Quicksand* by Nella Larsen**

protagonist in *Quicksand,* who looked white but was legally Black, reflected the author's own racial confusion. It is possible that at some times Nella herself may have passed for white. Nella also explored issues of women's sexuality and power in this groundbreaking book. Her second novel, *Passing,* focuses on the issues of dark-skinned versus light-skinned Black people. In her novel, as in the real world, light-skinned Blacks had leading roles in all levels of Black society, while dark-skinned Blacks felt discriminated against within their own race.

Her next work was a story that was later shown to be plagiarized, at least in part, although in 1930, she won a Guggenheim Fellowship, the first African American woman ever to do so. She went to Europe to work on her next novel, which was rejected by her publisher. After divorcing her husband in 1933, she disappeared from the literary scene and spent the next thirty years working as a nurse in Brooklyn. She never published another word.

BESSiE HEAD

Struggling Against Apartheid

BESSIE HEAD was the first "colored" South African writer to gain an international reputation. Her mother, Bessie Emery, was the daughter of a wealthy South African racing family. Her father was a Black stablehand who worked for them. The very existence of such a relationship was proof of insanity in apartheid South Africa, and her mother was committed to a mental hospital in Pietermaritzburg. Bessie Head was born in this asylum; her mother remained there until she died in 1943.

> Love is mutually feeding each other, not one living on another like a ghoul.
>
> **—Bessie Head**

Bessie was taken away from her mother at birth and placed in foster care, where she remained until she was adopted by a mixed-race family when she was thirteen years old. Her family sent her to mission schools.

In 1955 Bessie received her teaching certificate, but she found that she did not like teaching and quit after a few years, working instead as a journalist. In 1960 she married fellow journalist Harold Head. When they divorced in 1964, Bessie moved with their son to Serowe, Botswana. The move was motivated by her hatred of the apartheid system in South Africa as well as her search for personal peace.

In Botswana she began writing novels and short stories, many of them semi-autobiographical. Her stories dealt with discrimination, racism, poverty, and relationships. She wrote three novels; the best known was *A Question of Power,* written in 1973. They are all set amid the struggles and hardships of life for Black people in postcolonial Africa. Although she claimed to be nonpolitical, the subjects of her stories had heavy political significance, reflecting her own struggles with class, race, and apartheid.

MARGARET WALkER ALEXANDER

▲▲▲▲▲▲▲▲▲▲▲▲▲▲▲▲▲▲▲▲▲▲▲▲

Passionate Poet

BORN IN 1915, Margaret Alexander was a precocious youngster. She was reading at age four, finished high school at fourteen, and graduated from college at nineteen. She also started her career in poetry early on, at the age of eleven.

When she was sixteen, she met Langston Hughes, who was impressed with her poems and spent some time reviewing them with her and encouraging her to continue. She pursued her interest in poetry at Northwestern University, near Chicago, and was admitted into the Northwestern chapter of the Poetry Society of America. Some of her poetry was published in *The Crisis* magazine after W. E. B. Du Bois invited her to submit her writings. She also worked with the Federal Writer's Project, where she met Richard Wright, Arna Bontemps, and Gwendolyn Brooks.

Her master's thesis, completed at the University of Iowa, was a collection of poems titled *For My People,* which was published in 1942. It was the first volume of poetry by an African American woman published since 1928 and it won the Yale University Younger Poets Series Award. *Jubilee,* a novel about the Civil War–Reconstruction era, was her Ph.D. dissertation, published in 1965. She had worked on it for thirty years. *Jubilee* was translated into six languages and was also staged as an opera.

Walker also taught for many years at several colleges, including Livingston College in Salisbury, North Carolina, West Virginia State, and Jackson State in Mississippi; and she retired in the early 1990s. Most remarkably, she accomplished all this while supporting her family (her husband was disabled) and raising four children.

EDWIDGE DANTiCAT

Krik? Krak!

ENGLISH MAY BE Edwidge Danticat's second language, but her use of it has produced first-class work. Her father moved from Haiti to New York City in search of better work in 1971, when Edwidge was two. Two years later her mother left to join him, leaving Edwidge and her younger brother in the care of her paternal uncle in a poor area of Port-au-Prince. Literacy was low in Haiti, and the oral tradition of storytelling had an important place in the community.

Danticat grew up knowing loss and death. Both of her parents had left when she was very young, and under the dictatorial Duvalier regimes, people often disappeared for political reasons and were never seen again. The loss of her mother was very difficult for her, personally and socially. The phrase *sans manman* means "motherless" in Haitian, but is also a synonym for "hoodlum."

Danticat first demonstrated her penchant for writing at the age of seven. She borrowed the *Madeleine* books from her aunt and rewrote them with a Haitian heroine.

When she was twelve, she moved to New York City to rejoin her parents and to meet the two younger brothers that had been born there. The reunion was not easy for her. She felt that her parents and brothers were strangers. She had to learn English, and she was teased by her classmates, who called her a "boat person" because of her accent. Her parents enrolled her in a bilingual education program to help her make the transition.

She attended a high school geared for students looking toward a career in medicine. Her experiences there convinced her that nursing was not her calling. She continued her writing in high school, penning articles for the high school newspaper. One of those became the seed for her first novel.

After high school, she attended Barnard College on a scholarship, majoring in French literature. She received a B.A. in 1990, and was again considering nursing as a career. Partially this was because her parents encouraged their children to enter the professions. A career in the arts did not fit into that category. The quandary was resolved when Danticat won a scholarship to Brown University, where she enrolled in their graduate writing program. She sent her Brown thesis to a literary agent, who met with her a week later. That thesis, begun as an article in her high school paper, became *Breath, Eyes, Memory,* and was published in 1994. Critically acclaimed, it won her comparisons to Alice Walker.

This initial success was followed in 1995 with the publication of

Krik? Krak, a book of stories in the storytelling tradition she had grown up with in Haiti. In fact, the title is taken from the would-be storyteller asking her audience, "Krik?" which means, "Would you like me to tell you a story?" and the audience's reply of "Krak!" which means, "Yes, please go ahead!"

In these first two books, Danticat mined a lot of personal territory. Her next book, *The Farming of Bones,* was based on an historical incident. In 1937, anti-Haitian propaganda in the Dominican Republic resulted in the deaths of thousand of Haitians who were trying to enter that country to "farm the bones," a colloquial expression for harvesting sugar cane.

She was catapulted to national fame in 1998 when *Breath, Eyes, Memory* was selected as a book club selection by Oprah Winfrey. Soon readers everywhere knew about the alienated little girl who had arrived in New York City with no English but who went on to become the first African Haitian female author to write in English and be published by a major house.

CAROLiNA MARIA de JESUS
▲▲▲▲▲▲▲▲▲▲▲▲▲▲▲▲▲▲▲▲▲▲▲▲▲
Voice of the Favela

BORN TO A poor Black farming family in 1914 in rural Brazil, Carolina Maria de Jesus was lucky enough to have a mother who cared about education. Although illiterate herself, she forced

Carolina to attend school, even though she could attend for only two years. In those two years, Carolina learned the rudiments of reading and writing and continued to teach herself as best she could. Later Carolina moved to São Paulo, living in a *favela* (shantytown) with her three children. She collected paper from the garbage, which she sold to junkyards in order to feed her children.

She began to keep a diary in old notebooks she found. She wrote of the struggles of her daily life, but she also wrote poems and stories. In 1958, a Brazilian reporter visiting the slums talked to her and found out about her diaries. He asked to see them and was impressed with the power of her writing. Excerpts were published in his newspaper, and two years later the diaries were published as a book, *Quarto de Despejo* (*Beyond All Pity*). Carolina became a celebrity overnight. The first printing of 10,000 copies sold out in three days; 90,000 copies had been sold six months later. It remained on the bestseller list in Brazil for two years and, at this date, has still sold more copies than any other book in that country.

As a result of her writing, Carolina briefly became a darling of the Left, but they soon found that she was not

I don't know how to sleep without reading. I like to leaf through a book. The book is man's best invention so far.

—**Carolina Maria de Jesus**

interested in politics or fighting for change. She also was apparently not a very charming person, and she alienated many potential allies with her "difficult" personality. She was Black and a woman, and therefore people expected her to be grateful and docile. She was neither. She published four more books, but none were successful and she faded back into obscurity and poverty. She died in 1977.

ALICE CHILDRESS

Playwright, Actress, and Novelist

ALICE CHILDRESS spent her early years in Charleston, South Carolina, then lived in Harlem, New York, with her grandmother. It was her grandmother who actively encouraged her to write, prodding her to put down on paper her observations of people passing by their window.

Alice dropped out of high school, and while holding down several jobs, including that of governess, insurance agent, and machinist, in 1941 she began acting at the American Negro Theater in Harlem. She stayed with the company for eleven years, acting with Ossie Davis, Ruby Dee, and Sidney Poitier.

> My writing attempts to interpret the "ordinary" because they are not ordinary. Each human is uniquely different. Like snowflakes, the human pattern is never cast twice. We are uncommonly and marvelously intricate in thought and action, our problems are most complex and, too often, silently borne.
>
> **—Alice Childress**

Her first play, *Florence*, written in 1949, was well received, as were her next few plays. Her 1955 *Trouble in Mind* made her the first woman to win an Obie Award for the best original off-Broadway play. Later in her career she began writing plays for children and also fiction for adults and children. Her most controversial children's story was *A Hero Ain't Nothin' but a Sandwich*, which was published in 1973 and told the story of a thirteen-year-old heroin addict. Several school libraries banned it, even though it won several national awards and was named one of the Outstanding Books of the Year by the *New York Times Book Review*. It was later made into a movie starring Paul Winfield and Cicely Tyson. Alice continued writing fiction until 1987, when she returned to playwriting with a play called *Moms*, a tribute to Black comedian Jackie (Moms) Mabley.

Her pioneering work as an actress, playwright, and novelist paved the way for the likes of Lorraine Hansberry. Alice delved deeply into many controversial issues affecting the Black community, looking at the lives of everyday people struggling with oppression, racism, poverty, and drugs.

CHARLOTTA SPEARS BASS

Pioneering Publisher

IN 1910, Charlotta Spears was thirty years old and had been working at the *Providence Watchman* since she was twenty. Her doctor told her it would be best for her health if she moved west and rested a while. She took part of his advice, moving to Los Angeles, California, but she had a little trouble with the "rest" part. She took a part-time job selling subscriptions to the *Eagle,* the oldest African American newspaper in the West; two years later she owned the paper, functioning as both publisher and managing editor.

Feeling the need for some assistance, she formed a union with Joseph Bass, who had been cofounder of the Topeka *Plaindealer.* He became both the editor of the paper and her husband. They ran the paper together until his death in 1934, using it as a platform for social protest. After his death, Spears ran it alone for the next two decades.

Her community involvement did not end with the paper. She ran for a Los Angeles city council seat in the 1940s and served as western regional director of Wendell Wilkie's 1944 presidential campaign. In 1948, she was a founding member of the Progressive Party, and in 1952, she became the first African American woman to run for vice president of the United States. She and her running mate, civil liberties lawyer Vincent Hallinan, didn't win, but they certainly raised issues that mattered to them and their party—stopping the Korean War, stopping the Cold War, and banning the bomb.

In 1951, she sold the paper, but continued to work in politics the rest of her life. She was one of many who were persecuted during the McCarthy era witchhunts of the 1950s. She worked tirelessly against racism and sexism and was a leader in the peace movement until she died in 1969.

Win or lose, we win by raising the issues.
—**Charlotta Spears Bass**

JAMAiCA KINCAiD

A Unique Voice

SHE WAS BORN Elaine Potter Richardson on the Caribbean island of Antigua. Her family was loving but poor—they had no electricity, no running water, and no bathroom. One of her jobs as a young girl was to carry water in buckets from the public pump twice a day.

When she was nine years old, her mother had the first of Elaine's three siblings. Up until that point, Elaine had enjoyed a very close relationship with her mother, but now her mother's attention turned to her younger brother. The loss of her mother's attention affected her deeply. She became withdrawn and sullen. At the same time she was becoming aware that she and her people were subjects of British rule. This knowledge added to her resentment.

At the age of seventeen she had the chance to leave Antigua and took it, taking a job as a nanny in Scarsdale, New York. She completely cut herself off from home, not writing and refusing to open letters sent to her. When she left her job in Scarsdale, she did not leave a forwarding address and did not return to Antigua for nineteen years.

She moved from Scarsdale to New York City, taking another job as a nanny. For three years she took care of the family's four children and attended community college classes at night.

In 1970 she won a full scholarship to Franconia College in New

Hampshire, but returned to New York City after one year. In 1973 she changed her name to Jamaica Kincaid, saying it was "a way for me to do things without being the same person who couldn't do them—the same person who had all these weights." The name change was one way of finding and redefining herself. Another was the unique wardrobe she adopted, wearing jodhpurs and boots while walking the streets of Harlem, arriving at the Algonquin Hotel in plaid shorts and saddle shoes, or leaving her apartment wearing white pajamas and a seersucker bathrobe.

She began to make friends in the New York literary community. One of them was a contributor to *The New Yorker*'s "Talk of the Town" column. She began to accompany him as he researched his pieces, and he began to include some of her observations in his columns. Eventually *The New Yorker*'s editor asked her to write her own piece. She submitted notes, thinking he could craft it into a column. Instead the notes were published verbatim. That was the beginning of four years as a regular contributor to *The New Yorker*.

GERTRUDE MOSSELL: FIRST BLACK COLUMNIST

Born in 1855, Gertrude Mossell was part of the prominent free-Black elite of Philadelphia for ninety-two years. One of her cousins was Paul Robeson. After graduating from Philadelphia's "colored" schools, she was a schoolteacher for seven years. She began a career as a journalist, addressing issues of women's rights and social reform, a few years after her marriage. Her essays appeared in numerous newspapers and periodicals; she also wrote two books. She was one of a handful of African American women journalists when she began writing her column, "Our Woman's Department," in December 1885 for the *New York Freeman*. In her column she supported women's suffrage, business training for women, and racial equality.

Americans find difficulty very hard to take. . . .
I think life is difficult and that's that. . . . I am
interested in pursuing a truth, and the truth
often seems to be not happiness but its opposite. . . . The other strange thing is that, whatever I say in my writing, in my personal life I'm
really incredibly lucky. I suppose that's what
gives me the freedom to express negatives.

—**Jamaica Kincaid**

Then she began writing fiction. Her first story was published in *The New Yorker* on June 26, 1978. By 1983 she had published her first book-length short story collection, which won the Morton Dauwen Zabel Award from the American Academy and Institute of Arts and Letters. She followed with another book of short stories and her first novel, *Lucy.* Next was *Autobiography of My Mother.* Her first works were clearly cathartic in nature, exploring the wounds of childhood and the search for identity and self-worth in the world. She has said, "I'm just one of those pathetic people for whom writing is therapy."

In 1995 she resigned from her staff job at *The New Yorker* after almost twenty years. She was not happy with the direction the new editor was taking, saying the magazine had become "a version of *People* magazine." That same year she found out that one of her brothers in Antigua was dying of AIDS. Although she barely knew him, she returned to Antigua to be with him and repair the relationship. Her latest book, *My Brother,* tells the story of that reconciliation. Unfortunately, her relationship with her mother has not improved over the years. But her personal life seems happy. She married the son of William Shawn, the former editor of *The New Yorker,* and lives an idyllic life in North Bennington, Vermont, with her husband and two children.

EYES ON THE PRIZES

The controversial novel *The Color Purple* won the Pulitzer Prize for fiction in 1983, making its author, Alice Walker, the first Black woman to capture this prestigious award. Toni Morrison followed with a Pulitzer of her own for *Beloved,* and then trumped that by becoming the first Black person of either gender to win the Nobel Prize for literature in 1993.

Gender Benders,
Fabulous Firsts,
and other
Outrageous Ladies

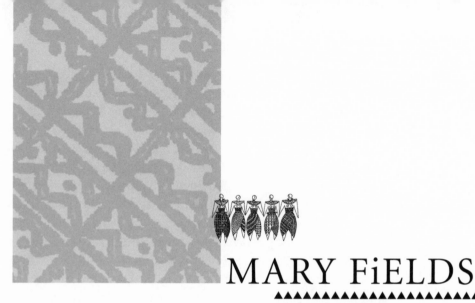

MARY FiELDS

▲▲▲▲▲▲▲▲▲▲▲▲▲▲▲▲▲▲▲▲▲▲▲▲▲▲▲▲▲▲▲▲▲▲▲▲

Stagecoach Mary

A BOUT ALL WE know of the first fifty-plus years of Mary Field's life is that she was born a slave somewhere in Tennessee around 1832. In 1884 or 1885, she surfaced in Toledo, Ohio, working as a general handywoman in a convent run by the Ursuline order, although how she came to be there is the subject of conflicting stories. During her tenure there, she met Mother Amadeus, head of the convent, and became her close friend.

Some years later, Mother Amadeus was ordered to St. Peters, Montana, to establish a school for Indian girls. Mary remained in Toledo, but when word reached her that Mother Amadeus was dying of pneumonia, Mary immediately left for Montana to care for her friend. Mother Amadeus recovered and Mary remained to work at the mission. She performed odd jobs, including tending the garden, doing light construction on the new convent building, and hauling the mission's freight. Her hauling duties required her to drive a stagecoach from Cascade to St. Peters, a distance of twenty-one miles each way, sometimes in severe weather. More than once she had to spend the night on the road, stuck in snowstorms and occasionally threatened by wolves.

Mary was a formidable woman, standing six feet tall and weighing 200 pounds. She worked hard, was a crack shot, smoked cigars, regularly carried a revolver and a rifle, and took stuff from nobody. She rubbed some people the wrong way, including the area bishop. She had several run-ins—one of which resulted in a little gunplay—with men hired by the convent. Although Mary didn't wound the man, he did hightail it out of that part of the country. Another time she stoned a man who stuck his tongue out at her. The bishop was incensed at her unwomanly behavior and ordered Mother Amadeus to fire her. Unbelievably, given Mary's devotion, the nun capitulated (granted, the bishop had ultimate authority over all the nuns in the convent) and after ten years of unpaid labor, Mary was out on her ear, broke and homeless.

Although forced to comply with the bishop's order, Mother Amadeus did her best to assist Mary in finding other employment and even helped her set up an eatery in Cascade. Mary's restaurant went broke twice because she was too generous with credit. Then Mother Amadeus helped her get another job, and in her sixties Mary became the second American woman to be a letter carrier. For eight years, Mary carried mail from Cascade to the mission, never missing a day. If the coach broke down, she would carry the mail on her back. If a train was late arriving at Cascade, she would sleep in the station until its arrival.

In 1903, Mother Amadeus was given a new post in Alaska. Mary, now seventy-one, stayed behind. She decided to give up the letter-carrying business and, moving into Cascade, began to take in laundry. This was her occupation for the next nine years. Once, she happened across a customer who had neglected to pay his bill, and decked him on the spot, announcing to onlookers that his account was now paid in full.

In spite of her eccentricities, the townspeople loved her. She smoked cigars until the day she died and had special permission from the mayor to drink in the saloon with men—a privilege extended to no other woman. Because she wasn't certain of her correct birthday, she celebrated several times a year, whenever she felt the need, and the school system would shut down to celebrate with her. When her laundry burned down in 1912, the town donated the necessary money and materials to rebuild it.

In her last years, Mary spent her time baby-sitting and supporting the local baseball team. She made boutonnieres for the team members from flowers in her garden, and rewarded them with bouquets when they hit home runs. When she died in 1914, almost the entire town turned out for her funeral. She was buried at the foot of the mountains she had grown to love.

CHARLoTTE RAY

Legal Eagle

CHARLOTTE RAY wanted to practice law, but she had a problem—she was a Black woman and it was 1869. She did have the determination she inherited from her father, Charles Ray, editor of the *Colored American* and pastor of Bethesda Congregational Church in New York, who was also known for his work on the Underground Railroad.

After college and a stint of teaching at Howard University, she began to take law classes and graduated from the Howard University Law School in February 1872. Rules for admission to the bar had been set by the Supreme Court of the District of Columbia. Under those rules, because she had graduated from Howard University Law School, she was not required to take a bar examination. Her application went through without a ripple, and Charlotte was admitted to practice in the lower courts of the District of Columbia in March 1872 and then to practice in the Supreme Court of the District of Columbia in April 1872.

She promptly opened a law office in Washington, hoping to specialize in real estate law, a field that did not require trial appearances. She was not able to build up sufficient clientele due to prejudice and also the economic depression of the time, so she was forced to give up active practice. However, she made history as the first Black woman regularly admitted to the practice of law in any jurisdiction in the United States.

MARY SEACoLE

▲▲▲▲▲▲▲▲▲▲▲▲▲▲▲▲▲▲▲▲▲▲▲▲▲▲▲▲

The Black Florence Nightingale

WE'VE ALL HEARD of Florence Nightingale, but Mary Seacole was an equally important figure in the establishment of modern nursing. She was born in the early 1880s in Kingston, Jamaica, to a free Black woman and a Scottish army officer. Her mother taught her two things: Creole medicine and hotelkeeping. She grew up happy and was well educated.

In 1836 she married Edward Seacole. He died shortly afterward, but during their short marriage they traveled around the Caribbean and Central America. After his death she returned to Kingston. Her mother died shortly after her return, and Mary took over running the boardinghouse. She lived independently for the rest of her life.

Mary Seacole

The hotel was destroyed in the great Kingston fire of 1843, but Mary rebuilt. During two epidemics of cholera and one of yellow fever, she sharpened her medical skills, and, trying to learn more about the disease, performed a postmortem autopsy of a baby who had died of cholera.

I made up my mind that if the army wanted nurses, they would be glad of me, and with all the ardor of my nature, which ever carried me where inclination prompted, I decided that I would go to the Crimea; and go I did, as all the world knows.

—Mary Grant Seacole

When her brother moved to New Granada, now the countries of Colombia and Panama, Mary followed, practicing nursing and establishing hotels in Cruces, Gorgona, and Escribanos. When she heard about the Crimean War, she traveled to England to offer her services to the British Army. She was refused because of her color. But Mary was determined to help and paid her own way to the Crimea, a 3,000-mile journey.

There she located Florence Nightingale, and again offered her services. She was rebuffed again, so Mary decided to build her own "hotel for invalids." The British Hotel, which she built at Spring Hill near Balaclava, became a center for both officers and soldiers even though she did not allow drunkenness or gambling. She dispensed medicine, meals, and the occasional entertainment, tending to the wounded on the battlefield under fire and making "home visits" to campsites.

The venture was a financial disaster, and she ended up spending her savings to obtain necessities and medicines. When the war ended in 1856, she was deeply in debt, but she was also widely acclaimed in the newspapers. William Howard Russell, an influential journalist, wrote of her, "I have witnessed her devotion and her courage . . . and I trust that England will never forget one who has nursed her sick, who sought out her wounded to aid and succor them, and who performed the last offices for some of her illustrious dead." Her autobiography, *The Wonderful Adventures of*

Mrs. Seacole in Many Lands, became a bestseller, releasing her from bankruptcy.

Mary was awarded the Crimean Medal, the French Legion of Honor, and a Turkish medal. She spent the rest of her life traveling between London and Kingston. She died in 1881 and is buried in London.

MARiE LAVEAU

▲▲▲▲▲▲▲▲▲▲▲▲▲▲▲▲▲▲▲▲▲▲▲▲▲

Voodoo Queen

MARIE LAVEAU was not one person but two, a mother and daughter. Both became legendary voodoo queens in New Orleans. The mother, a free woman, was a quadroon, the daughter of a wealthy

ELIZABETH LANGE: SISTER NUN

During the Haitian revolution, Elizabeth Lange fled Cuba for the United States in 1817 and settled in Baltimore in 1827. Despite heavy opposition to the education of Blacks, she opened the first school for Baltimore's French-speaking Black immigrants. Because of her work in education and her service to the church, Pope Gregory XVI approved her request to organize the Oblate Sisters of Providence Order, which was the first Black Roman Catholic order to operate in the United States. Mother Mary Elizabeth, as she was known, became the first superior-general. During the Civil War, she was the head of St. Benedict's School and later helped establish many other schools in Baltimore, Philadelphia, and New Orleans. By the time of her death, the Oblate order had spread across the United States and into the Caribbean and Central America.

white planter and a mulatto woman. In 1819 she married Jacques Paris, a free man of color who was a native of Santo Domingo. She worked as a hairdresser, a profession that gave her access to the gossip and secrets of her patrons. It is said that she also made her money through blackmail and procuring light-skinned Black women for wealthy white men.

Eventually, she left Jacques and began living with Louis Christophe Duminy de Glapion, with whom she had fifteen children. She practiced voodoo, a blend of African religious beliefs and Catholicism. Her followers believed that she could cure the sick, bring luck with her amulets, and see into the future. By 1830 she was the preeminent voodoo queen of New Orleans, the voodoo capital of the world at the time. People in the city, both Black and white, including politicians and policemen, were terrified of her power. She retired in 1869 and died in June 1881, having passed the family business on to her daughter, who had been born in 1827. The second Marie was as notorious as the first. Other voodoo queens followed them, but none attained their notoriety or power.

LULU WHiTE

▲▲▲▲▲▲▲▲▲▲▲▲▲▲▲▲▲▲▲▲▲▲▲▲▲▲▲▲▲▲▲

Legendary Madam

STORYVILLE, AN AREA encompassing two city blocks around Basin Street, was a notorious red-light district in New Orleans in the late 1800s, and one of its most notorious madams was Lulu White. She was born on a farm near Selma, Alabama, and arrived in New Orleans in the 1880s. She was arrested repeatedly for prostitution, disorderly conduct, and white slavery.

Although not very attractive, being rather short and dumpy, White was able to attract a string of influential and wealthy men through other talents she possessed. A shrewd businesswoman, she parlayed her acquaintance with them into a four-story marble monument, a magnificent house of ill repute that she named Mahogany Hall. It had five parlors and fifteen lavishly decorated bedrooms. White was so powerful in city circles that her $40,000 establishment was assessed at only $300.

She was known for descending the staircase, drowning in diamonds—including those studding her teeth—while singing her favorite song. She wore diamond rings on all ten of her fingers, bracelets up both arms, a diamond necklace, a tiara, and an emerald brooch on her chest, and topped it all with a bright-red wig. It has been rumored that Mae West's character in the movie *The Belle of the Nineties* was modeled after Lulu, except, of course, that Mae's character was white.

White's pimp, or "fancy man," George Killshaw, stayed with her for twenty-five years, until he was able to relieve her of a chunk of her cash in one fell swoop. In 1906, wanting to invest some of her fortune, White traveled to Hollywood, California. She went in her usual luxurious style, she and George traveling in a private railroad car with servants to attend to their every desire. Her plan was to buy real estate and production facilities, and perhaps star in a movie or two herself. She returned to New Orleans to finalize her plans. The next year she sent George back to California to consummate the deal for land and equipment. However, she made one small miscalculation. She sent George with all of the necessary funds in cash, some $150,000. She never saw George, or her money, again.

This mistake was not the end of Lulu White. In 1908 she built a saloon next to Mahogany Hall to serve as a kind of retirement fund. Mahogany Hall operated until 1917, when Storyville was closed by federal order. Here history loses track of Lulu White. There are plenty of rumors but no hard facts. A teller at the Whitney National Bank of New Orleans reported that she made a withdrawal in 1941, but what became of her after that remains a mystery.

WiLLA BROWN
AND JANET BRAGG

▲▲▲▲▲▲▲▲▲▲▲▲▲▲▲▲▲▲▲▲▲▲▲▲▲▲▲▲▲▲

Flying High

BESSIE COLEMAN may be the best-known Black aviatrix, but she was not the only pioneering Black woman to take to the skies. Willa Brown followed in her mighty footsteps and left a mark of her own. Willa was born on January 22, 1906, in Glasgow, Kentucky, but was raised and went to school in Indiana. She attended Indiana State Teachers College and graduated with a B.A. in 1927. Willa then married and became a teacher, but changed her mind about both.

She had heard about the exploits of Bessie Coleman, and in 1932 she left the teaching profession, divorced her husband, and moved to Chicago to pursue her interest in flying. There Willa gained the assistance of *Chicago Defender* editor Robert Abbott, who had been instrumental in Bessie Coleman's decision to go to France to get her pilot's license. Abbott was financing tours in which African American aviators visited African American colleges and universities to encourage young people to get into flying. Willa enrolled in the Aeronautical University in Chicago, earning a Master Mechanic certificate in 1935. In the next four years she received her commercial pilot's license, an M.B.A. from Northwestern University, her private pilot's license with a near-perfect score, and her Civil Aeronautics Administration ground school instructor's rating.

She married Cornelius Coffey, her instructor at the Aeronautical University, and together they founded the Coffey School of Aeronautics in 1938. Willa handled administrative duties as well as teaching. In the 1930s, she was part of the struggle to have Blacks included in the Civilian Pilot Training Program (CPTP) and the Army Air Corps.

In 1939 Congress authorized the admittance of African Americans into the civilian flight training programs. Willa became the coordinator for the CPTP in Chicago, and the Coffey School of Aeronautics was awarded a government contract to train pilots. Between 1938 and 1945 they trained about 200 flyers, some of whom later became part of the 99th Pursuit Squadron at Tuskegee Institute, better known as the Tuskegee Airmen.

Among her other accomplishments, Willa became the first

African American officer in the Civil Air Patrol, attaining the rank of lieutenant. She was also the only woman in the United States holding both a mechanic's license and a commercial license in 1943. As the cofounder of the National Airmen's Association of America, she taught aviation subjects for the Works Progress Administration Adult Education Program and in 1940 was chosen by the U.S. Army Air Corps to conduct experiments for the admission of Black aviators into the U.S. Army Air Corps. Later in life she taught aviation in high schools and spread the gospel of flying on the Cleveland-based *Wings over Jordan* radio show.

Janet Bragg, a contemporary of Willa Brown, made an impact in both aviation and nursing. She was born March 24, 1907, in Griffin, Georgia, near Atlanta, and was the youngest of seven children. Her family was of African American, Cherokee, and Spanish descent. Traditionally her family attended Tuskegee Institute, but she opted to attend Spelman College in Atlanta instead.

Janet graduated with an R.N. degree and soon after moved to Rockford, Illinois, to live with an older sister. She worked as a supervising nurse and attended Loyola University at night, earning a graduate certificate in public health administration. Janet worked for a dentist, a general practitioner, and an eye, ear, nose, and throat specialist while she did graduate work in pediatric nursing. In 1933 she was working for the Metropolitan Burial Insurance Company as a health inspector. In 1951 she married Sumner Bragg, whom she had met at Metropolitan. Together they established two nursing homes for elderly Black people.

While continuing her nursing career, Janet also pursued her interest in aviation. She had been inspired by a roadside billboard she saw that said, "Birds learn to fly. Why can't you?" but she was unable to get into an aviation school. At the time, Bessie Coleman notwithstanding, Black Americans were considered to be mentally and physically incapable of piloting airplanes.

Finally Cornelius Coffey and John Robinson, two Black men who in 1928 had both graduated with distinction from Chicago's Curtiss Wright School of Aeronautics, were enlisted by the aeronautics school as instructors as long as they would recruit African Americans. Janet Bragg was the only woman in their first class of twenty-seven students. The second semester, three more women joined her. In 1933, this group built an airport and hangar together, and Bragg bought the first airplane, which she shared with the others in return for maintenance. She helped to set up an interracial coeducational flight school, although she met continuing opposition to her career in commercial and military aviation.

During World War II, Janet applied to work with the Women's Auxiliary Service Pilots transporting military aircraft to England. They accepted her application and then told her they didn't know what to do with a Black woman. Even though she was well educated, a registered nurse, and a licensed pilot with her own plane, she was eventually rejected because of her race.

Not one to give up, she then went to Tuskegee, Alabama, where Black male pilots were being trained, and tried to earn her commercial certificate. Previously, in Chicago, she had passed all the requirements except her flight test because of bad weather. But the white examiner in Alabama refused to certify her. No Black woman had been given a commercial license in Alabama, and he wasn't about to make her the first. Undeterred, Janet returned to Chicago, took her flight test, and received her certification within a week.

When a call was put out for 60,000 more nurses for the military nurse corps, Janet once again tried to help in the war effort. She was told that the quota for Black nurses had been filled.

Even though Janet wasn't able to serve in the war, she had accomplished a great deal for the cause of Blacks in aviation. She was a founding member of the Challenger Air Pilots Association, a national organization of African American aviators that was established in 1931, and she helped construct the organization's first airstrip in 1933. She was a founding member of the National Air-

MILDRED BLOUNT: HATTER TO THE STARS

Mildred Blount became interested in millinery while she was working as an errand girl at Madame Clair's Dress and Hat Shop in New York City. Soon she and her sister, a dressmaker, opened their own shop. Wealthy New Yorkers formed the clientele for their dresses and hats. Mildred was hired by John Frederics' Millinery of New York in the 1930s, and her career skyrocketed. She created an exhibition of hats based on designs from 1690 through 1900 that was shown at the 1939 New York World's Fair. Because of that exhibit, she was hired to design hats for the movie *Gone with the Wind*. Women like Rosalind Russell, Joan Crawford, Gloria Vanderbilt, Marian Anderson, and many wealthy Black women became her clients. One of her hats was featured on the August 1942 cover of *Ladies' Home Journal*. In 1943 she became the first Black American to have her work exhibited at the famous Medcalf's Restaurant in Los Angeles. During the late 1940s she opened a shop in Beverly Hills, but soon after she faded into obscurity.

men's Association of America, which sent representatives to Black colleges and universities to interest students in aviation. Additionally, she was among a group of Black pilots who flew the first memorial flight over Bessie Coleman's grave in 1935, an event that has become an annual tradition.

In 1984 the Civil Rights Division of the Federal Aviation Administration gave her an award acknowledging her role as a pioneer in Black aviation. In 1985 she received the Bishop Wright Air Industry Award for outstanding contributions to aviation. She is an active member of the Tuskegee Airmen's Association.

JOhNNETTA COLE

Sister Prez

WHEN JOHNNETTA COLE was growing up in Jacksonville, Florida, Mary McLeod Bethune, the famous educator, became one of her role models. Mary had been a friend of the family, and Johnnetta had visited her often. Having Mary as a model, combined with her family's emphasis on the value of education, it is no surprise that Johnnetta went into teaching. She was so facile in her studies that she entered Fisk University in Nashville, Tennessee, at the age of fifteen.

She loved Fisk for the exposure it gave her to Black intellectuals, but after two years she transferred to Oberlin College in Ohio, which her sister was attending. This was another world, very different from the Jim Crow South she had grown up in. She met people from all over the United States as well as from other countries. She also discovered cultural anthropology, which became her passion.

After Oberlin she attended Northwestern University, where she earned a master's degree and a Ph.D. She left Northwestern and began teaching anthropology and Black studies at Washington State University. From there she went to the University of Massachusetts and did fieldwork in Cuba, Haiti, Grenada, and Africa.

She was a full professor of anthropology and the director of the Latin American and Caribbean Studies Program at Hunter College in New York when she got the call that changed her life—she was a candidate for the presidency of Spelman College in Atlanta.

> Go out and make this a better world! Be involved!
>
> —Johnnetta Cole

Spelman, a 115-year-old Black women's college, founded as a school for freed female slaves, had had three white women and one African American man as president. Johnnetta would become the first African American woman to preside over this prestigious institution. Affectionately known as "Sister Prez" by the student body, Johnnetta's leadership has led Spelman to be ranked among the top liberal arts colleges in the nation since 1988. During her tenure, the school's endowment tripled to $128 million. Oprah Winfrey and Bill and Camille Cosby have been major contributors. She also instituted a community service program that was recognized as a "Point of Light" by former president George Bush, a corporate partnership program, and a mentorship program.

Cole retired from Spelman in June 1997. She now serves on the board of Coca-Cola. In May 1999, she was selected to receive the Radcliffe Medal in honor of her achievements.

BEATRiCE VORMAWAH
▲▲▲▲▲▲▲▲▲▲▲▲▲▲▲▲▲▲▲▲▲▲▲
A Sailor's Life

BEATRICE VORMAWAH, a petite young Ghanian, did not know how to swim as a child, and was not allowed to go near the water because her mother was afraid she would drown. In June 1995, even though as an adult she still did not know how to swim, she became captain of the 16,000-ton ship *Keta Lagoon* and the only female among Ghana's twenty-five ships' captains. Although she is only 5 feet tall and looks younger than her forty-plus years, she is firmly in charge of her all-male crew of forty-two.

She didn't set out to become a sailor. She had been planning a career in medicine, and enrolled in the merchant marine course as a diversion from the monotony of medical studies. "But once I got involved," she said, "that became my ambition—to go straight to the top."

Beatrice's accomplishments are that much more remarkable set in the context of a country that has very traditional male-female roles, where almost half of adult women are illiterate, and less than a third of the girls go beyond primary school. She says that despite the cultural conditions, she has never experienced

> We have to keep the fire burning. We've broken this barrier and we have to continue.
>
> **—Beatrice Vormawah**

hostility or discrimination, although she has encountered some difficulties due to African beliefs that a woman on a ship will drive the fish away or cause mermaids to create storms.

Most of her time is spent carrying cocoa beans, timber, and aluminum from the port of Tema, near Accra, to Great Britain, a twenty-four-day round trip. Because of her job, her domestic life is also untraditional. She is married and has three children, but her husband takes care of the children while she goes off to sea.

Someday, she says, she will get a shore job and give up sailing, but she plans to continue urging other African women to break out of their traditional roles.

BARbARA HARRiS

Pioneering Prelate

Barbara Harris surmounted both racism and sexism to become the first woman bishop in the Episcopal Church. She was born June 12, 1930, in Philadelphia, Pennsylvania. She was active in her local Catholic parish, forming a young adult group that quickly became the largest in Philadelphia. After graduation from high school, she went to work for a public relations firm. She remained active in her church, participated in the St. Dismas Society, a prison-visiting group, and did volunteer work in prisons for fif-

238

teen years. Harris then moved to a public relations position at Sun Oil Company, while becoming a board member of the Pennsylvania Prison Society.

In 1968 Harris moved her church membership to the North Philadelphia Church of the Advocate. That year a group of Black Episcopal ministers formed the Union of Black Clergy, later to become the Union of Black Episcopalians. Harris, along with several other women, lobbied for membership and was accepted. When the church approved the ordination of women, Harris began to study for the ministry.

Barbara Harris

Her first post after her ordination in 1980 was as priest-in-charge at St. Augustine of Hippo in Norristown, Pennsylvania. After four years, she became the executive director of the Episcopal Church Publishing Company. Her subsequent election as suffragan bishop of the diocese of Massachusetts was quite controversial. The obvious objections were that she was female—although the church had opened all orders to women thirteen years before—and that she was divorced, although there had been divorced male bishops before. More to the heart of the matter was probably

> I could be a combination of the Virgin Mary, Lena Horne, and Madame Curie and I would still get clobbered by some.
>
> —**Barbara Harris**

her social activism. She advocated the rights of women, the poor, and ethnic minorities. Many people were uncomfortable with someone so outspoken. The appointment stood, making her the first Black woman bishop in the worldwide Anglican community.

ACKNOWLEDGMENTS

This book would have remained forever a project for "someday" without the support, love, and badgering of the following people:

My mother, Alice Simms, who brought me into the world and made sure that I was somewhat literate. She is herself a heroic Black woman;

My husband, Tim Smith, who has always known I am a writer, even when I didn't;

My son, James Patterson, for making me work when I didn't want to;

My sister, Jeanette Madden, who created the magnificent cover and who has known me all my life and still speaks to me;

Claudia Schaab, for gently nudging me;

Nina Lesowitz, the best gossip buddy anyone could ask for;

The entire staff of Conari Press who have blessed me with their talents: Don McIlraith, Mignon Freeman, Teresa Coronado, and Heather McArthur (founding members of the Conari Lending Library), Everton Lopez, Sharon Donovan, Leah Russell, Rosie Levy, Jenny Collins, Suzanne Albertson, Claudia Smelser, Brenda Knight, and Will Glennon (Dr. Kindness). My special thanks to Mary Jane Ryan, friend and editor extraordinaire, who believed so wholeheartedly in this project and me; and to Leslie Berriman who did the final shaping and whom all you readers must thank for making sure I was coherent on paper (keeping me coherent in daily life is too big a job for anyone).

PHOTOGRAPHY ACKNOWLEDGMENTS

24: Denver Public Library, Western History Collection; **35, 71, 90, 156, 162, 191, 201, 210:** Archive Photos; **75:** Moorland-Springarn Research Center Howard University; **108, 124:** Marine Biological Laboratory; **133, 142:** Associated Press (AP); **183:** Schomburg Center for Research in Black Culture; **225:** The National Library of Jamaica; **239:** Bachrach Photography

RECOMMENDED READING

Altman, Susan. *Extraordinary Black Americans.* Chicago: Children's Press, 1989.

Anderson, Martha. *Black Pioneers of the Northwest 1800–1918.* Martha E. Anderson, 1980.

Ballenger, Seale. *Hell's Belles.* Berkeley, CA: Conari Press, 1997.

Bolden, Tonya. *The Book of African-American Women.* Holbrook, MA: Adams Media Corporation, 1996.

Busby, Margaret. *Daughters of Africa.* New York: Ballantine Books, 1992.

Dirie, Waris, and Cathleen Miller. *Desert Flower.* New York: William Morrow and Company, Inc., 1998.

Franklin, John Hope, and August Meier. *Black Leaders of the Twentieth Century.* Chicago: University of Illinois Press, 1982.

Harris, Joseph E. *Pillars in Ethiopian History.* Washington, DC: Howard University Press, 1974.

Hine, Darlene Clark, Elsa Barkley Brown, and Rosalyn Terborg-Penn. *Black Women in America.* Bloomington, IL: Indiana University Press, 1993.

Jackson, Guida M. *Women Who Rule.* Santa Barbara: ABC-CLTO, Inc., 1990.

Katz, William Loren. *Black People Who Made the Old West.* New York: Thomas Y. Crowell Company, 1977.

Keckley, Elizabeth. *Behind the Scenes.* Chicago: R. R. Donnelley & Sons Company, 1998.

Kessler, James H., J. S. Kidd, Renee A. Kidd, and Katherine A. Morin. *Distinguished African American Scientists of the Twentieth Century.* Phoenix, AZ: Oryx Press, 1996.

Levine, Robert M., and Jose Carlos Sebe Bom Meihy. *The Life and Death of Carolina Maria de Jesus.* Albuquerque, NM: University of New Mexico Press, 1995.

Liswood, Laura A. *Women World Leaders.* San Francisco: Pandora, 1995.

Litwack, Leon, and August Meier. *Black Leaders of the Nineteenth Century.* Chicago: University of Illinois Press, 1988.

Lunardini, Christine. *What Every American Should Know About Women's History.* Holbrook, MA: Adams Media Corporation, 1997.

Phelps, Shirelle. *Contemporary Black Biography.* Detroit, IL: Gale Research, 1997.

Rake, Alan. *Who's Who in Africa.* Metuchen, NJ: The Scarecrow Press, Inc., 1992.

Rose, Al. *Storyville, New Orleans.* Tuscaloosa, AL: University of Alabama Press, 1974.

Sertima, Ivan Van. *Great Black Leaders: Ancient and Modern.* n.p.: Journal of African Civilizations Ltd., Inc., 1988.

Smith, Jessie Carney. *Powerful Black Women.* Detroit, IL: Visible Ink Press, 1996.

Stephens, Autumn. *Wild Women.* Berkeley, CA: Conari Press, 1992.

_____. *Wild Women in the White House.* Berkeley, CA: Conari Press, 1997.

Sweetman, David. *Women Leaders in African History.* Oxford, England: Heinemann International, 1984.

Thurman, Sue Bailey. *Pioneers of Negro Origin in California.* San
Francisco: Acme Publishing Company, 1971.
Ventura, Varla. *Sheroes.* Berkeley, CA: Conari Press, 1998.

INDEX

ABOUT THE AUTHOR

Annette Madden lives in Oakland, California, with the most wonderful husband on Earth (which means he tolerates all of her nonsense) and her "baby" boy, who is twenty-one and has given up on convincing his mother that he is now an adult. She is a history buff and an avid science fiction fan.

Don McIlraith

TO OUR READERS

CONARI PRESS publishes books on topics ranging from spirituality, personal growth, and relationships to women's issues, parenting, and social issues. Our mission is to publish quality books that will make a difference in people's lives—how we feel about ourselves and how we relate to one another. We value integrity, compassion, and receptivity, both in the books we publish and in the way we do business.

As a member of the community, we sponsor the Random Acts of Kindness™ Foundation, the guiding force behind Random Acts of Kindness™ Week. We donate our damaged books to nonprofit organizations, dedicate a portion of our proceeds from certain books to charitable causes, and continually look for new ways to use natural resources as wisely as possible.

Our readers are our most important resource, and we value your input, suggestions, and ideas about what you would like to see published. Please feel free to contact us, to request our latest book catalog, or to be added to our mailing list.

2550 Ninth Street, Suite 101
Berkeley, California 94710-2551
800-685-9595 • 510-649-7175
fax: 510-649-7190 • e-mail: conari@conari.com
http://www.conari.com